International Perspectives of Crime Prevention 13

Contributions from the 28th German Prevention Congress

Eds.
Erich Marks, Dr. Claudia Heinzelmann, Prof. Dr. Gina Rosa Wollinger

With contributions from:

Inès Amzal, Carlotta Bauer, Caroline L. Davey, Alexander Fekete, Manuela Freiheit, Friedrich Gabel, Christoph Gusy, Tjorven Harmsen, Rita Haverkamp, Dagmar P. Heinrich, Claudia Heinzelmann, Chris Hetkämper, Christoph Kowalewski, Francesc Guillén Lasierra, Erich Marks, John Rook, Pilar De la Torre, Andreas Uhl, Macarena Rau Vargas, Gina Rosa Wollinger, Andrew B. Wootton, Andreas Zick

Forum Verlag Godesberg GmbH 2025

Bibliographic information published by the German National Library

The German National Library lists this publication in the Deutsche Nationalbibliographie: detailed bibliographic data are available in the Internet at
http://dnb.d-nb.de

Editing and layout: Pascal Specht
Coverdesign: Konstantin Megas, Mönchengladbach

Print: Libri Plureos GmbH, Friedensallee 273,
22763 Hamburg

ISBN: 978-3-96410-051-1 (print)
ISBN: 978-3-96410-052-8 (eBook)

Content

Introduction

This thirteenth edition of "International Perspectives of Crime Prevention" includes a selection of the outcomes of the 16th Annual International Forum (AIF) of the 28th German Prevention Congress. The 28th German Prevention Congress took place in Mannheim on 12 and 13 June 2023 and brought together around 2,500 people from the field of crime prevention and related areas in Germany and worldwide.

The main topic of this congress was "Crisis & Prevention". The "Mannheim Declaration", which emerged from the debates and expertises, is presented first.

Part I presents four of the eleven scientific expertises that were prepared in the run-up to the congress. They examine the main congress theme from different professional perspectives.

Part II contains five further essays, which report on lectures of the congress and deal with topics such as urban safety and feelings of insecurity as well as prevention of corruption and the link between poverty and crime.

We would like to thank all the authors for their contributions.

The German Prevention Congress is an annual event that takes place since 1995 in different German cities and targets all areas of crime prevention: Administration, youth welfare, the judiciary, churches, local authorities, the media, politics, the police, crime prevention committees, projects, schools, the health system, organisations, associations, and science. The desired effect is to present and strengthen crime prevention within a broad societal framework. Thus, it contributes to combating crime and reducing the risk of becoming a victim. In addition, this is associated with reducing the fear of crime among the population.

The main objectives of the congress are:

- Presenting and exchanging current and basic questions of crime prevention and its effectiveness
- Bringing together partners within the field of crime prevention
- Functioning as a forum for the practice of crime prevention and for fostering the exchange of expertise

- Helping to get into contact at the international level and to exchange information
- Discussing implementation strategies
- Developing and disseminating recommendations for practice, politics, administration, and research in the field of crime prevention.

Since its foundation, the German Prevention Congress has been opened to an international audience with a growing number of non-German speaking participants joining. Because prevention is more than a national concern and should be focused internationally this step seemed crucial. To give the international guests a discussion forum, the Annual International Forum within the German Prevention Congress was established in 2007. This event offers lectures in English language as well as other activities within the German Prevention Congress that are translated simultaneously. In 2012 the DPT-Institute for Applied Prevention Research (DPT-I) was founded. It promotes the dialogue between prevention research, practice, and politics, by offering further events, online-seminars and by participating in (international) research projects.

We hope to find a broad audience, interested in the upcoming events of the German Prevention Congress. For more information, please visit our website at www.praeventionstag.de/go/en.

Claudia Heinzelmann, Erich Marks, and Gina Rosa Wollinger

The German Prevention Congress – DPT
and the permanent partners DFK, ProPK, WEISSER RING

Mannheim Declaration
28th German Prevention Congress

Crises & Prevention

The 28th German Prevention Congress focuses on the omnipresent topic of multiple crises and poses the question of the contribution of prevention in terms of both preventing and overcoming crisis situations. Based on the debates at the congress and a comprehensive accompanying publication containing eleven expert opinions from various disciplines[1], the 28th German Prevention Congress, together with the partner organisations Stiftung Deutsches Forum für Kriminalprävention (DFK), Polizeiliche Kriminalprävention der Länder und des Bundes (ProPK) and WEISSER RING e.V., is issuing this 'Mannheim Declaration'.

A crisis is a phase in which serious changes are emerging, but it is still unclear whether a catastrophe will occur. Whether a phenomenon is assessed and perceived as a crisis arises in social interaction, is changeable and is experienced subjectively in different ways. We are currently facing several crises at the same time: climate change, the COVID-19 pandemic and war, including in Europe, as well as their consequences: extreme weather conditions, economic downturn, inflation, refugee movements, increasing social inequalities, among others.

It is currently of particular importance that an accumulation of crises is being recognised and that these harbour systemic risks. They therefore jeopardise the system as a whole and are characterised by high complexity, cascading effects and tipping points, among other things.

Prevention in the context of a crisis does not just mean trying to prevent a crisis from occurring in the first place. The term resilience is often used here, which refers to dealing positively with crises that have already occurred. It is essentially about strengthening resistance. Prevention in this sense takes place at an individual, communal/organisational and societal level.

---

1 See page 25 in this book

Prevention at the level of individual coping with crises

- The ability to cope positively with crises in terms of individual resilience is supported by protective factors on a biopsychosocial level. These factors must therefore be specifically considered and promoted. Good experiences and support in this area can prevent crises from leading exclusively to uncertainty, disorientation and feelings of loss of control.
- In particular, a child-centred and personality-strengthening up-bringing provides a solid 'foundation', which makes it easier to cope with stressful situations in adulthood. Children who grow up in difficult circumstances should therefore be supported by paying particular attention to building relationships in education and leisure activities.
- In times of crisis, there is usually a lack of clear concepts based on sound knowledge. Here it is important to be able to deal with divergent views and unclear situations. This ability is referred to as ambiguity tolerance and refers to the ability to endure and accept contradictions, ambivalence and ambiguity. As a central competence, the appropriate handling of different scientific statements, i.e. a trained categorisation of opinions, sources and findings, should also be specifically promoted.
- The sooner people understand the cause-and-effect relationships between events, the better they can deal with crises. If they then see opportunities for action for themselves, they can experience 'selfefficacy' and realise that their actions bring about positive change. This is an elementary need, the fulfilment of which contributes to an active and positive approach to crises. Where possible, appropriate options should therefore be identified.
- If there is a lack of understanding of the crisis, which is particularly the case with systemic crises, there is an increased attribution of blame to 'the foreigner'. Prejudice and discrimination are on the rise. Here, it is important to prevent anti-democratic and radical groups from using these moments in a targeted manner to offer affiliations and identifications with disinformation and conspiracy narratives and thus expand their influence.
- The experience of distributive justice is also highly relevant, as the feeling of being a 'crisis loser' can have similar consequences. In this context, the problem of the loss of solidarity and devaluation of socially weak groups can be observed.
- Crises also represent a major psychological burden for those affected. Offers for recovery and for stress and anxiety regulation can be very

helpful here. Mental health support should be seen as a cross-cutting issue in crisis prevention and be located in various areas of society. Offers can range from counselling and sports activities to the design of green spaces close to residential areas.

Prevention at the level of organisational risk prevention and municipal crisis management

- At a local level, strengthening local social communities is of central importance. It has been shown that an optimistic self-perception of social cohesion in one's own neighbourhood increases the willingness to help in the event of a crisis.
- Seeing oneself as a community and being able to pursue a goal together is what constitutes local social capital. A high level of social capital is an important preventative factor. Municipalities can identify differences in this respect in the neighbourhoods and should therefore specifically promote social capital in the less advantaged neighbourhoods.
- Based on their general willingness to help, the population should be empowered to play an active role in dealing with and overcoming crises. The concept of 'community resilience' is based on the collective capacity of the population and does not view them as passive and worthy of protection alone, but rather ascribes an active role to them.
- The easier it is to understand the causes of crisis events and the options for action, the easier it is to manage them. However, this is particularly challenging in the case of systemic crises due to their complexity. Crisis communication plays a particularly important role here with the task of making the events comprehensible and explaining solutions and measures. There is still a need for optimisation in terms of the organisation and coordination of communication.
- An effective crisis management culture promotes both broad and subject-specific work. It requires both the ability to think in an integrative and cross-sectoral manner and access to specialised technical knowledge. The basis for this is the transparent exchange between those responsible across institutions. Internal communication based on trust must leave room for controversial discussions and alternative solution options.
- Organisational resilience means being able to adapt to changes and crises, cope with them and emerge stronger. To this end, public

authorities, companies and other organisations must have mechanisms and strategies in place to deal with unforeseen events and adapt their business processes, structures and resources accordingly. Resilient organisations establish a culture of learning and adaptation in which mistakes are seen as learning opportunities and innovative, forward-looking solutions are promoted.

- To safeguard critical infrastructure in particular, local authorities should be aware of the key local players. Communication chains, crisis teams (with assigned responsibilities) and emergency plans should be prepared preventively. The relevant areas must have been identified and the processes rehearsed in order to be able to react appropriately immediately.

Prevention at the level of society as a whole

- Identifying and dealing with crises is based on subjective assessments and is linked to certain values and norms. Political actors should be aware of this when making decisions in response to a crisis and discuss it transparently. For example, the necessary assessment of which groups and individuals are particularly vulnerable in crisis situations must be communicated in a comprehensible manner.
- In crises, existing social imbalances and disadvantages become even more apparent and tend to intensify. A good social policy is therefore also a fundamental component of preventive crisis management.
- The complexity of current crises means that there are often differing assessments from (scientific) experts. From a decision-theoretical perspective, it is not advisable to simply follow the prevailing opinion. Rather, the risk or the extent of damage must be considered if the minority opinion is right and nothing is done. This must be weighed up against the prevention costs. Against this background, it can also be rational to follow minority opinions.
- Crisis prevention must weigh up how high the costs of prevention are and put this in relation to the risk. Opportunity costs may also be incurred here if other areas could be neglected as a result of prevention work.
- Last but not least, it is necessary to give the actors involved in crisis management the opportunity to reflect on their handling of the crisis. The appropriate resources must be made available for a critical examination of the chosen structures, processes and measures and their ongoing optimisation.

Expertises

Gina Rosa Wollinger

Introduction

> *"Which events and developments are perceived at all and described as crisis-like does not lie in the things themselves, but is something (socially) made."*

Climate change, the Corona pandemic, the Russian war of aggression against Ukraine - current societal challenges with all their consequences (drought, refugee movements, hunger, energy shortages, etc.) are often described as crisis-like. Crisis phenomena are omnipresent in public debates, the subject of the political agenda and tangible in their consequences in the everyday lives of many people. The impression of living in a time characterised by crises in particular is likely to be created primarily by the multitude and rapid succession of crisis events: No sooner does the danger of the Corona pandemic seem to have been averted, than the next one follows with the Ukraine war and its crisis-like consequences (energy crisis, etc.). Crises not only replace each other, but also overlap. Discussions about the right way to deal with crisis phenomena thus necessarily also result in weighing and prioritising measures to regulate crises, for example in the debate on whether longer nuclear power plant lifetimes and a reactivation of coal-fired power plants are justified to contain the energy crisis, despite the ongoing climate crisis.

Against this background, the impression of living in particularly crisis-ridden times seems understandable. And yet it would not be the first time that a year or a decade of crisis has been proclaimed (see e.g. Prisching, 1986, p. 15 ff.) and Olaf Scholz would not be the first to be dubbed crisis chancellor. Or to put it another way: the feeling of living in particularly crisis-ridden times is not new, even if the objects of crisis sometimes diverge (for example, economic and financial crisis). Reinhart Koselleck, who has had a decisive influence on the theoretical discussion of the term, writes: "In our century there is hardly an area of life that does not receive its decisive accents with the help of this term" (2004 [1982], p. 617).

1. Genesis of the Concept

The term "crisis" is not new, but can already be found in antiquity, where it is originally located: The Greek word krísis is translated here as divorce, decision, judgement or turning point (see, among others, Graf, 2020, p. 18; Koselleck, 2004 [1982], p. 617 f.). In ancient Greece, the term belonged to a legal context in which crisis was understood as a decision in the sense of "reaching a verdict and passing judgement" (Koselleck, 2004 [1982], p. 618). Furthermore, there is an early use of the term in medicine. It refers to the phase of the course of a disease that constitutes the turning point: either recovery or chronification up to death (Graf, 2020, p. 18; Koselleck, 2004 [1982], p. 619; Steg, 2020a, p. 425). Likewise, a theological use is found in relation to the "last decision" of the Last Judgement (Koselleck, 2004 [1982]; Steil, 1993, p. 20).

The transfer of the concept of crisis to other areas of society took place in the course of the 17th century and significantly in the 18th and 19th centuries. The transfer to economic circumstances (economic crises) was important for the further establishment of the term (Koselleck, 2004 [1982], p. 641). One of the first to use the term in its current sense was Jean-Jacques Rousseau, who not only associated it with a turning point between the original order and death or catastrophe, but also with the "(...) possibility of something new and a better and higher social order" (Steg, 2020a, p. 420). The emergence of various theories of the state revealed a new understanding and analysis of society, into whose toolkit the concept of crisis was inserted. However, the attempts to interpret social change were not solely influenced by the multitude of political, social and economic upheavals, but were primarily due to the fact that changes were perceived as such. The perception of crises as situations with an open outcome goes hand in hand with an understanding of the world that is less based on religious or other metaphysical ideas, but in which the human being, as an acting actor, moves to the centre of the explanation. In this respect, "'crisis' becomes a structural feature of the modern era" (Koselleck, 2004 [1982], p. 627). Modernity is thus characterised by crises and crisis considerations. This way of dealing with social developments forms the basis of a new scientific discipline, sociology. In this respect, it is not surprising that Auguste Comte, one of the founding fathers of sociology, used the concept of crisis to describe social developments (Steg, 2020a, p. 426) and that sociology is also referred to as the science of crises, which attempts to record social changes and upheavals descriptively and to explain their causes.

2. Current Understanding of Crisis and Topicality

The current semantics of the term refers to a period of time or phase in which a (serious) change is imminent, but it is still open how it will take place. Thus, there can be a massive deterioration of the situation, a continuation of the initial situation or an improvement (hence the idea of crisis as opportunity). The crisis is thus characterised by the fact that a problem of whatever kind exists and a strong change in the initial situation is indicated or is already occurring, but the further development is still undetermined. The crisis is thus not deterministic, it is a "caesura with an open outcome" (Steg, 2020a, p. 431), and in this respect differs from the catastrophe, in which the emergency has already occurred.

Bösch et al. defined crisis "(...) as the broad public perception of threatening societal challenges that demand immediate fundamental decisions and changes to solve them" (2020, p. 5). In addition to emphasising the characteristics of urgency and the need for decisions, this description also refers to a subjective element of crises with the term "perception". Crises as phases of social, political or economic upheavals and turning points are not objectively identifiable or given. Thus, although a crisis composite (e.g. energy crisis) may be widely represented in public discourse, the crisis still contains "disparate meanings, affect dispositions and problem situations" (Steil, 1993). Which events or changes and at what threshold something is called a crisis is the result of processes of perception and definition and thus varies subjectively (Bösch et al., 2020, p. 5ff.; Steg 2020a, p. 424). Whether, for example, an increase in migration to Germany is conceptualised as a crisis depends on the respective interpretation of this circumstance. Climatic changes are not a crisis per se, but only become one when their extent leads to further changes (extreme weather events, etc.) and this is perceived as threatening or a pressure to act to prevent worse. Crises are thus socially constructed (Graf, 2020; Steg, 2020a). Which events and developments are perceived at all and described as crisis-like is not in the things themselves, but is something (socially) made. In this respect, there are divergences between different societies, but also within a society, as to what is to be assessed as a crisis, what in particular expresses the character of a crisis and what measures are to be taken. The decisive factor here is also who or which social groups have the authority to interpret a certain circumstance and who is recognised as an expert. The relationship between subjective perception and objective circumstances can take on different constellations: "Crisis-like processes do not always have to lead to a state of consciousness of the individuals affected that corresponds to the objective circumstances; likewise, any subjective moods of crisis do not always have to have grown on the basis of real threatening circumstances" (Prisching, 1986, p. 26).

When crises are described as a characteristic of the modern era, this is not (necessarily) to be understood as meaning that it is the multitude of social, political and economic transformations that characterise this period. Likewise, societies before that experienced (sometimes serious) upheavals, even if the multitude and dynamics of changes sometimes extended over longer periods of time. Crises as a characteristic of the modern era rather mean the fact that phenomena are perceived primarily as crises: "In modernity, crisis diagnoses are in fact permanently in vogue" (Steg, 2020a, p. 424). The concept of crisis thus also serves as a "category of analysis" (Steg, 2020a, p. 425) or an "instrument of observation" (Bösch et al., 2020, p. 5ff.) of social, political or economic changes, and they often intertwine.

It should be taken into account here that the attractiveness of the concept of crisis, however, is not only due to its suitability for present-day analyses, but also to its alarming character (Steg, 2020a, p. 424). Discussing circumstances in connection with the concept of crisis creates a "pressure to act" (Bösch et al., 2020, p. 6) or represents an "imperative to act" (Graf, 2020, p. 20), now having to make the right decision. In this respect, the concept of crisis is also suitable for political instrumentalisation.

3. Crises as a loss of normality

Even if crises are seen as an essential feature of modernity and the omnipresence of crises is often emphasised, this does not immediately lead to the conclusion that crises or experiences of crises are normal. Crises describe a circumstance that represents a "non-intended deviation from normality" (Steg, 2020, p. 430). Rather, the permanent presence of crises should rather be understood as "normal anomalies", as Steg (2020b) calls it: It is not the crisis itself that is normal, but the occurrence of crises. Crises are characterised precisely by experiences of (threatening) loss of normality. According to Lessenich (2022), social normality consists of three components: an empirical one (what people do), a normative one (what people should do) and an evaluative/legitimising one (how people evaluate it). Normality is produced again and again in everyday life. In this process, not all members of society participate equally in normal living conditions; rather, it is the so-called middle class of society that functions as the "instance of normalisation" (Lessenich, 2022, p. 36). For Lessenich (2022), the serious upheavals, changes or the need for change, one could also say crises, of our time are to be located in the economy, migration, the handling of finite resources and in the context of the so-called identity politics debate, which in turn give rise to a more or less diffuse feeling that everything is somehow no longer normal. In this context, it is above all the people who previously participated in normal living conditions or circumstances who now feel the "consequences that shatter normality" (ibid., p. 10). This in turn is reflected in "irritation and need for reassurance" and the "search for identity confirmation" (ibid., p. 17) as expressed, for example, in the form of outrage over "gender gaga" and "veggie days". Crises and their consequences affect members of society to different degrees and in different ways. Instead of asking about the effects of crises on individuals and society, one could ask the other way round what happens to a society that loses its identity-forming normality. Lessenich states that the current German society despairs of the fact that it "(...) cannot hold the old and think the new (...)" (2022, p. 37). In view of the current crises or transformations, basic "normal" practices and certainties will, for various reasons, no longer be possible.

Further crises are to be expected in the future and even if crises and perceptions of crises are not a unique feature of the 21st century, but rather a characteristic of modernity, as explained above, the "accumulation of crises" (ibid., p. 122) is nevertheless a defining feature of our time. The intensity and frequency of phenomena defined as crises in recent times, which are not only the subject of a wide variety of debates but have also led to noticeable changes for many people in their everyday lives, establish a special "crisis topicality".

4. Crises and Prevention

Against this background, the thematic focus of the 28th German Prevention Congress entitled "Crises and Prevention" asks about the role and the possibility of prevention in the context of crises. Explicitly, this is not about a specific subject of crises, but about general characteristics of crisis phenomena. In this respect, the question of generalisability arises first: can an "essence" of crises be identified, circumstances and characteristics that are inherent in every crisis, even though every crisis has its "specific logic and momentum" (Steg, 2020a, p. 430)? Crises are dynamic. Which phases or cycles of crises can be meaningfully distinguished from one another? How do crisis situations or phases affect individuals and society? It is known from research on violence, for example, that in conflict situations it is not so much the internalised values and norms that explain people's violent behaviour, but that violence arises from situations (Eckert & Willems, 2002). To what extent do crises cause violent or, in a broader sense, anti-social behaviour among people? Or does a crisis lead to more cohesion in a society? Crises mean uncertainty, everyday life can be massively affected. How does the loss of experiences of normality affect not only society as a whole but individuals?

Furthermore, it is questionable what is meant by prevention in this context. Does preventive action in relation to future crises mean trying to maintain the status quo? With regard to the fact that current economic and life styles are the cause of climate change, this does not seem to be an appropriate understanding of prevention for all crisis phenomena. To what extent does prevention in the context of crises also mean forms of transformation and adaptation? What is the significance of the much-discussed concept of resilience or transformative resilience?

If crises mean a situation "(...) in which the decision is due but has not yet been made" (Koselleck, 2004 [1982], p. 619), this ultimately raises the question of the agency: who is called upon to act preventively and to what extent? Crisis prevention can take place on different levels and covers a wide field. "Crisis competence" can include psychological factors of resilience as well as political-democratic action competencies and municipal crisis management (civil protection, preparation for black-out scenarios, crisis communication, etc.).

5. The expert reports

Eleven expert reports on the 28th German Prevention Congress will cover the diverse field of prevention in connection with crises. They will go beyond the original topic of the German Prevention Congress, violence and crime, and ask about the effects and connections of crises on society as a whole and the significance of prevention in this context. The expert articles take an interdisciplinary perspective by looking at the topic from a sociological, legal, psychological and philosophical point of view as well as from the perspective of risk and crisis management or civil protection.

There are English versions of four expert articles in this publication. These are briefly described below.

In the first contribution, Rita Haverkamp, Christoph Gusy and Tjorven Harmsen take an interdisciplinary look at the phenomenon and trace the social process of the crisis, ask about the challenges for democracy and the rule of law and address the effects and requirements for municipalities, which have to deal with the consequences at the operational level. The special nature of current crisis situations is described by the existence of multiple crises with an "unbounded" character. Prevention in relation to crises should not only be designed to avoid crises, but should also explore the possibilities of resilient handling. In this context, dealing with uncertainties and crisis communication are of particular relevance.

The effects of crises on extremist attitudes and actions are described in the article by Manuela Freiheit, Andreas Uhl and Andreas Zick. Times of crisis are characterised by insecurity and the experience of loss of control, which in turn influence anti-democratic tendencies and group-based misanthropy. It shows how social groups deal with this and to what extent feelings of insecurity and the need for orientation can be instrumentalised for certain purposes. The article examines the question of how the findings of research to date can be used for prevention.

Another article analyses crisis phenomena from a philosophical perspective. Friedrich Gabel examines the significance of concepts of values and normality for the classification of phenomena as crises and the derivation of measures. In doing so, he emphasises the social construction of normality and the identification of and dealing with dangers. This differs within society. In this respect, crises are both evaluated and understood differently. Furthermore, the consequences of crises are not the same for everyone. Crisis prevention should take into account these divergences in values and notions of normality within society.

Furthermore, the expert reports explicitly refer to the topic of crises and prevention at the municipal level, which must primarily take operative action in times of crisis. In their contribution, Alexander Fekete, Chris Hetkämper and Carlotta Bauer explain the understanding of resilience in the context of civil protection and municipalities. They emphasise the relevance of networking, exchange and participation of cities and municipalities, which should not only be implemented in times of acute crisis, but on a permanent basis. The article argues for a certain culture of dealing with crises at the municipal level. This includes, among other things, including formats for the participation of the population more strongly in the future and also taking them into account in crisis communication.

References

Bösch, F., Deitelhoff, N., Kroll, S. & Thiel, T. (2020). For reflexive crisis research - an introduction. In F. Bösch, N. Deitelhoff & S. Kroll (Eds.), Handbook of crisis research (pp. 3-16). Springer VS.

Eckert, R. & Willems, H. (2002). Escalation and de-escalation of social conflicts: The road to violence. In W. Heitmeyer & J. Hagan (Eds.), International handbook of violence research, (pp. 1456-1480). Westdeutscher Verlag.

Graf, R. (2020). Between motivation to act and experience of powerlessness - The transformation of the concept of crisis in the 20th century. In F. Bösch, N. Deitelhoff & S. Kroll (Eds.), Handbook of crisis research (pp. 17-38). Springer VS.

Koselleck, R. (1982). Crisis. In O. Brunner, W. Conze & R. Koselleck (Eds.), Geschichtliche Grundbegriffe. Historical lexicon on political-social language in Germany (pp. 617-650). Vol. 3. Klett-Cotta.

Lessenich, S. (2022). No longer normal. Society on the verge of a nervous breakdown. Hanser Berlin.

Preunkert, J. (2011). The crisis in sociology. Sociology, 40(4), pp. 432-442.
Prisching, M. (1986). Crises. Böhlau.
Steg, J. (2020a). What does crisis actually mean? Sociology, 49(4), pp. 423-435.
Steg, J. (2020b). Normal anomaly. The Corona crisis as caesura and opportunity. Blätter für deutsche und internationale Politik, 65(6), pp. 71-79.
Steil, A. (1993). Crisis semantics. Sociological studies of knowledge on a topos of modern contemporary experience. Leske + Budrich.

Rita Haverkamp, Christoph Gusy, Tjorven Harmsen

Crises and their prevention from an interdisciplinary perspective[1]

> *"Considering prevention as part of the crisis management cycle means overall: accepting that crises will continue to occur."*

1. Introduction

The 21st century is characterised by crisis. The term encompasses various events of different duration and scope ("financial crisis", "refugee crisis", "climate crisis") and is currently experiencing an almost inflationary use. Crisis can be described as a "catch-all term" that loses contours. Present times are marked by continuously generated crises. They form an "amorphous meta-crisis" as "a catastrophe without an event because it consists precisely in continuity, in the sheer continuation. It has no clearly identifiable actors and culprits, no precise moment or definable location, no single scenario - rather many, large and small, clear and unclear, probable and improbable moments, localities and courses" (Horn, 2014, German in original). The multifaceted nature of the phenomenon, of which causes are often negotiated globally and in an (inter)national context, creates a variety of complex and sometimes almost unmanageable challenges for municipalities at the local level. The climate crisis and the crises caused by the Russian invasion into the Ukraine (e.g. "energy crisis") are current examples of this.

---

1 The general understanding of crisis in this article as well as the findings from the crisis management literature study are largely based on a collaboration with Prof Dr Oliver Ibert at the Leibniz Institute for Research on Society and Space (IRS) in Erkner, Germany. We would therefore like to express our heartfelt thanks to him.

The joint project "Legitimation of Emergencies - Changes in Legitimation in Emergencies" (LegiNot), which has been funded by the German Federal Ministry of Education and Research (BMBF) since March 2022, focuses on the Covid-19 pandemic as an example of a permanent crisis, for which no "script" for management was available, and which has deepened existing distortions in society over time, with which municipalities are particularly confronted. The joint research group first deals with theoretical issues surrounding the definition of the terms "disaster", "crisis" and "emergency". In this paper, the theoretical focus is on the crisis and its prevention from an interdisciplinary perspective. Starting from an understanding of crisis as a social process, the focus will be on the legal state of emergency and then on its significance for municipalities. Following from this, prevention in times of crisis is subjected to special requirements.

2. Crisis as a social process

2. 1 General definition criteria: Threat, urgency, and uncertainty

Anyone looking for an unambiguous definition of a crisis may quickly be disappointed in the scientific literature. The term crisis is used very frequently without agreement on what it is supposed to denote (cf. Steg, 2020; Preunkert, 2011). There is a lack of demarcation within the individual disciplines as well as it is not always indicated when, for example, the term is only being used strategically (to signal the significance of a particular topic).

We would therefore like to concentrate first on a term from crisis management research, which provides a clear initial definition. A relevant quotation is often used here to describe acute crisis situations. Crisis is defined in terms of the three characteristics of threat, urgency, and uncertainty: as a "serious threat to the basic structures or the fundamental values and norms of a system, which under time pressure and highly uncertain circumstances necessitates making vital decisions" (Rosenthal et al., 1989, cited in Boin et al., 2018, p. 24).

This definition suggests that crises are decision-making situations ("making vital decisions") in which the above-mentioned characteristics of threat ("serious threat"), urgency ("time pressure"), and uncertainty ("uncertain circumstances") come together. In most cases, the experience of the threat acts as a trigger: it quickly becomes clear to those involved that immediate action is necessary to avert further escalation. However, it is unclear exactly how to act. In the acute crisis, therefore, "motivation to act and the experience of powerlessness" come together (Graf, 2020, German in original).

Two aspects already become clear with this definition. (1) On the one hand, it reflects a general understanding of crisis, which is independent from the concrete situation on which it is based. Whether it is flooding in the Ahr valley (which happened in Germany 2021), the spread of the SARS-CoV-2 virus or a gas shortage: decisions always have to be made under conditions of threat, urgency, and uncertainty. This general understanding is also called "all-hazards approach". (2) On the other hand, the focus shifts towards the social system, which experiences the crisis as a decision-making situation in itself. There is no crisis "out there" (cf. Spector, 2019), but it becomes a social and communicative process (cf. Voss & Lorenz, 2016), in which not only decision-makers and crisis managers, but society in general can be involved.

2. 2 Transgression of boundaries as a feature of today's crises

Crises today occur not only with greater frequency, but also with a changed quality. Scientists and practitioners (for example, in civil protection) find it increasingly difficult to mark the beginning and end of a crisis. This applies to the spatiality of crises, when global interdependencies of, for instance, economy or politics mean that crisis phenomena can no longer be confined locally. Today, crises are also difficult to define temporally – they begin subtly and, as the Covid-19 pandemic shows, cannot be clearly defined in their ending. This happens even more so, when the management of the consequences of crises as well as the side-effects of measures must be counted as part of crisis management. The causes and effects of today's crises extend far into space and time. Crisis management literature, the characteristic of "transgression of boundaries" is used to describe this new quality. Ansell et al. (2010), for instance, speak of "transboundary crises": Today's crises transcend established spatial boundaries, for example of nation states, sectors, individual organisations, or knowledge domains. With regard to the temporal transgression of boundaries, there is a discourse on "permanent" or "creeping crises" (Boin et al., 2021).

The transgression of boundaries in today's crises brings special challenges for all those involved. In most cases, many actors are affected at the same time. Depending on the frame of reference the crisis encounters (e.g. public administration or business enterprise), it is processed according to specific logics (cf. Nassehi, 2021; Brinks & Ibert, 2021). These forms of processing can differ greatly and offer particular potential for conflict. In Germany, for example, at the beginning of the Covid-19 pandemic, there was widespread criticism of the "patchwork quilt" that resulted from different regulations by the federal states. Crises that transcend borders call for "collective action", but at the same time raise problems of coordination and centralisation of decision-making competencies (cf. Ansell et al., 2010). For the crisis managers involved, this entails particular coordination problems.

The transgression of boundaries also makes the communication and justification of measures to the population a more complex matter. In clearly delineated emergency operations – such as an accident on the motorway – operational measures are almost self-explanatory. Usually, bystanders will gratefully accept the presence of emergency forces such as police, fire brigade and rescue units, since it is obvious that quick measures must be taken, for instance to rescue people from a burning car, without putting material assets first. In transboundary situations, however, such a clear picture is no longer given. Transgressing crises experience a complex social negotiation. They bring together different stakeholders, interest groups, but also different levels of consternation. For many people, they are not immediate experiences, but rather experiences mediated by the media – and yet they also participate in the interpretation and negotiation of crises. Research therefore addresses the importance of media reporting or the use of media, social networks, etc. (cf. Jarren & Neuberger 2020).

Over the course of time, contradictions and conflicts of objectives can unfold from these different participations, bringing with them unpredictable dynamics of their own and not least also influencing the perception of the crisis situation in the population. In transboundary crises, there is no "one" acute peak that could be quickly combated with targeted measures. The threat is much more diffuse and has acute peaks as well as weakened phases (cf. Ibert & Harmsen, 2022, p. 11). Measures taken are no longer self-explanatory, especially in crises that have no clear temporal limits, but require greater justification and explanation to the outside world. The population becomes an active part in the negotiation of crisis management.

2. 3 Understanding crisis as a social process

Crisis is therefore not a "state in itself", but a process of social negotiation. Crises and also crisis concepts present themselves differently depending on the reference system and their logics. Reference systems can, for example, be organisations such as certain business enterprises or authorities, hospitals, or courts. The legal system (chapter 3) as well as municipalities (chapter 4) as reference systems of crisis will be addressed separately. Particularly in transgressing crises, there are interdependencies between the various systems involved, which can strengthen or weaken the crisis dynamics (cf. Homer-Dixon et al., 2022). Accordingly, the Covid-19 pandemic, for instance, does not exist as "the one crisis", but becomes an umbrella term for a wide variety of crisis dynamics occurring simultaneously.

Such an understanding of crisis as a social process goes beyond the definition of purely subjective criteria of a crisis on the one hand and purely objective criteria on the other. Wolfgang Bonß (2021) distinguishes between three waves in risk and security research, which can likewise be applied to the version of crises (cf. Voss & Lorenz, 2016). (1) The first wave consists of defining crisis on the basis of objective criteria. An example of this would be the scientific collection of data on the loss of biodiversity on earth or on global warming, which objectively define the "climate crisis". (2) A second wave, on the other hand, addresses the perception of crisis, and emphasises that it is not in linear relation to the objective data. According to this understanding, a climate crisis only exists if it is perceived as such by the population and decision-making systems. According to this understanding, crisis is a pattern of perception and interpretation, that is, it takes place equally "in the mind" of the observer (see also Gabel's contribution in this volume). (3) Only the third wave understands both criteria in a dynamic interrelationship. Trigger, perception, and negotiation criteria become intertwined over the course of the crisis. During the Covid-19 pandemic, infection figures can be measured objectively. The decisions made on the basis of these are the product of communicative negotiation and lead to desired effects (such as decreasing infection rates through the introduction of masks or lockdown), but also to undesired side effects (such as economic collapses and social polarisation), which are in turn responded to in the form of a crisis.

Understanding crisis as a social process, as in this third wave, means that there can no longer be a "view from above". Crises are linked to the experience of those involved and thus go beyond individual events (cf. Roux-Dufort, 2007, p. 110). In their contexts of origin, courses, and consequences, they are to be thought of as exclusively dynamic. They are processed and communicatively negotiated by society. And this also means that they do not have a central and superordinate structure of interpretation. For it is precisely modern society that is based on decentralised structuring. With it, there is no longer a centre from which crises can be viewed in a superordinate way (cf. Nassehi, 2021). Rather, crises arise in an overlapping dynamic of "involved participants", each with their own perspective (cf. Brinks & Ibert, 2021).

The following two chapters will describe what a crisis in law and its demands on municipalities actually means.

3. Challenges to Democracy and Law

3. 1 Crisis in law

In current German law, the concept of crisis is almost irrelevant. Its use in laws and other legal texts is remarkably low. There are terms with similar meanings, such as "state of emergency", "disaster" or "major damage event", which cover partially or completely the same phenomena. While allowing for situational as well as specific differentiation of possibilities, they are less usable as large-scale formulas. If the decade from 2010 to the present was a decade of crises, it was not therefore also a decade of states of emergency or catastrophes. These terms are not in themselves capable of capturing the entire spectrum of meanings the broad concept of crises entails.

Law recognises special challenges in the fact that special events pose special challenges. The crisis is an exceptional legal state, not the normal state. The exceptional situation is characterised by a special need for action, special expectations of competent bodies and the overtaxing of regularly responsible bodies. It therefore requires higher-level, including political, management or coordination. In short: a crisis shifts tasks and powers. But it is by no means only the much-cited "hour of the executive". Primarily responsible for eliminating the crisis are the people affected by it: They are guaranteed by constitutional law the primary experts for their own survival. In this sense, the disaster is the hour of the harmed people themselves. This gets overlooked in most legal discussions. Additionally, lawmakers may require them to take precautionary and preparatory measures in the general interest or in protection of third parties, for example by fulfilling vaccination obligations, self-protection of businesses, technical facilities, or processes, or building up emergency reserves. At the moment of crisis, everyone must evacuate, help, or make equipment available. Legally, these are no longer just rights, but also duties. They therefore require special legitimisation. Besides, crisis-management expectations are centrally directed at public authorities and their satellites. They are supposed and even held to be responsible by constitutional protective duties, to observe potential damage events, warning, providing resources, granting protection, organising consequence management, paying compensation and, if necessary, investigating responsibilities. And all this while responsible agencies are already overburdened. The resources to be managed are scarce almost by definition, and participation right and allocation procedures have to be organised and coordinated under conditions of overstress. None of this is only a responsibility of the executive. On the contrary: Necessity requires commandments, the constitutional regulations and guidelines of the Basic Law apply in special situations as well, albeit with certain modifications, which in turn are equally provided by the Constitution.

In this sense, the emergency is a stress test not only for executive powers, but also for parliaments, courts, and the constitution itself. They each have to cope with the crises in a manner that is specific to their function, with divided responsibilities. This requires law that is suitable for emergencies. It needs to provide sufficient governance and legitimacy under the crises' special conditions while still being sufficiently legitimate itself. Such laws should be enacted prior to the occurrence of the emergency when thorough and procedural consideration can be given. Here, we are faced with a first dilemma: the next emergency will happen eventually, but we just do not know in advance exactly when and how it will occur. There are individual emergencies with a "script" based on previous experience, which can and should be used as a reference. Other emergencies pose difficulties regarding the determination of their exact circumstances as well as their regulation – not least due to the aforementioned characteristic of dissolving boundaries. They have no "script". This requires forecasting competencies, which legislatives and jurisprudence have in no greater means than other disciplines involved. Interdisciplinary and interdepartmental cooperation is required here which can increase forecasting capabilities, but which according to previous experience cannot completely secure them. It is not only the recognition of danger that depends on the forecasts, but also the possibility of its prevention. Appropriate measures can only be taken if the phenomena to be prevented and the measures necessary to avert them are known at least approximately. While the police usually succeed routinely in averting dangers due to their longstanding experience with the law and knowledge of occurring dangers, this becomes more complex with an increasing transgression of boundaries, amount of affected people, difficulty in assessing the specific risk events and the necessary measures to manage them – including time, space, as well as their extent. Prevention competence asks about resource allocation and distribution competence. This differs from the normal governmental distribution procedures in particular by the suddenness of its occurrence, the scarcity of the available goods, at least at the actual place of damage, and the excessive demands on personnel and other resources, such as information. It also requires special regulations and special acceptance on the part of those affected.

Here the law is faced with a series of contradictory expectations. If it is enacted before the disaster, it can apply to all emergencies and all potentially affected persons including responsible authorities being able to prepare for it. But legislators do not know the concrete future emergencies. Therefore, we may find the risk of the legal standards not meeting the specific requirements of the individual case, because their content tends to be wide-meshed and general. The more wide-meshed regulations are, the more the task of legitimisation shifts towards the law-executing authorities, which have to specify indeterminate legal concepts or exercise discretion. The greater the need for conflict-solving law, the greater the danger that the law will not meet the increased requirements of the particular emergency. The text of the law is stable, but its application varies extremely and is therefore in need of legitimisation. In such cases more legitimacy tends to come from more precise rules. This is not generally inadmissible; the many amendments to the Infection Protection Act (IfSG) in Germany during the pandemic, for example, indicate this. However, such case-by-case motivated law is also case-by-case. There is a risk that it focuses too much on the acute situation and does not sufficiently take into account other or later challenges, due to the situational pressure to act. This results in the need for new, yet again case-specific law. The consequence might be self-replicating cascades of legislative changes motivated by heightened expectations and media attention hype which tend to follow rather than steer developments. This situation between the Scylla of too little and the Charybdis of too much is perceived as a problem not only by the legislators but also by the norm addressees. The abstract crisis law controls and relieves too little, the cascade of specific crisis law also controls too little and relieves too late. Its norms are untested and susceptible to change at short notice, sometimes they may even be out of force before they could actually be effectively enforced. This induces an additional stress test for the legitimation of the state and of democracy. However, this is not necessarily an insolvable dilemma since steering is not the only function of parliament. But there are further supplementary parliamentary and judicial functions that must also be operationalized. We should mention here legitimacy through control. Obviously, this is also subject to special conditions of execution: controllers should check, but not further overburden or even paralyse the already overburdened organs of action. This is known and recognised for normal cases but may require readjustments for emergency situations. The case of emergency changes the need of parliamentary steering and parliamentary control.

3. 2 Needs for legitimation in emergencies

Accordingly, the decisive legal functions in an emergency are steering, control and legitimisation. The latter has some specific features in special situations. At least four areas of specific legitimation needs can be distinguished.

(1) First of all, there is the warning. It links the announcement of an increased danger situation with requests for action, for example to take special safety measures, to evacuate an area or to no longer enter it. Although it does not create a legal obligation to act or to refrain from acting, it may entail legal disadvantages if the requested action is not taken. The request for action is the part that requires legitimisation. If the emergency situation already exists, it may legitimise itself. Otherwise, the request for action requires special legitimisation precisely because its object, the danger, has not yet occurred. The minimum requirement is that the request unambiguous in terms of content and contains a clearly recognisable call to action for the addressees: Where to go when the sirens start wailing? Warnings must be given well in advance: if the disaster has occurred, warnings can at best be given of impending consequential damage. But it must also not be given too early and too often to avoid wear effects: Those who have taken refuge several times, even though there was no threat of damage in retrospect, will possibly no longer follow the warning the next time, even if there actually are dangers now.

(2) There are also emergency powers. They can be used immediately before, but also during the disaster, for example, to order those affected to provide assistance, stay out of restaurants or wear face masks. Such measures are commands and prohibitions and thus classic encroachments on fundamental rights. They can be legitimised in two ways: On the one hand "from above" by the law, insofar as it contains standards of action that are sufficiently well known. On the other hand "from below", i.e. through the enforcement staff in action with regard to those affected, insofar as administrative scope for action is used or not used. Both mechanisms follow different logics: the former being independent of individual cases, the latter being shaped and demanded by the individual case. And in case of the former, administrations and courts can relieve themselves by referring to the law; in case of the latter, they must bear the burden of legitimacy themselves in the absence of clear guidelines.

(3) Related to this is the third area, reasoning. To legitimise means to reason. This requires arguments. These can be expertocratic, referring to experts, specialist opinions or technical reasons, which may convince people who, for their part, accept expertise. Arguments may also be legal if reference can be made to soft law. They can ultimately be political, for example by referring to majorities or preliminary decisions, or gain acceptance through discussion and decision. All forms stand side by side: where a distinction can be made between "right" and "wrong", expertise is required; where "team caution" and "team easing" are opposed, because of expertise not at hand, political discussion can and must take place. Executives can hardly do this in individual cases due to their own lack of expertise. This makes public discussion in parliaments, the media, and the population itself all the more important. Reasoning cannot replace law, but it can help to make it more effective by increasing the willingness to follow or at least tolerate it. These interrelationships presuppose, in particular, that acting officials are convinced of the law that is to be enforced, of its legitimacy, and that they are prepared to risk conflicts with persons affected by it. The acquisition of legitimacy in the administration is enacted with regard to those, who later seek legitimation in front of the citizens.

(4) The fourth area is that of assigning responsibility. It regularly begins at a later time, when questions will be asked about shortcomings in light of the damage and failures. There are different processes by which responsibility is assigned: informally through administrative supervision, more formally through the initiation of disciplinary or even criminal proceedings, as well as through parliamentary committees, namely committees of enquiry. This also shows that the allocation of responsibility to be predominantly personal, not so much organisational, occasionally succeeding when someone gets punished. To this end, however, it follows different logics than the enforcement. In particular, the elements of personal attribution and culpability in German law are almost exclusively tailored to individual persons. This can happen retrospectively-sanctioning when past events are reviewed and judged. However, such processes can also have preventive effects if it becomes apparent that sanctions will also be imposed in case of repeated failure. However, the opposite may occur if no one wants to expose themselves in the next emergency in order not to incur responsibility.

The fields of action and legitimacy are comparatively clear. But the answers to many questions are still at the beginning. For example, the question, whether and, if so, why the need for legitimacy changes with the duration of an emergency. Certainly: An unresolved situation that has hardly been researched scientifically can be temporarily managed for reasons of caution, with reference to nature of individual measures. This is less likely to succeed in the case of longer-duration emergencies when there has been time enough to test legislative or administrative measures. But to what extent can habituation effects or the feeling that "nothing happened to me, and nothing will happen to me again" change the need for legitimacy? Media's communication of the emergency will also change, which only a few people are confronted close up. For the most of them the catastrophe is a media event. Emergencies create and focus attention, bundle topics and areas of discussion, and can trigger public debates. But sensations tend to wear out. Little research has been done on how the media deal with long-lasting emergencies, including the effects on its recipients. Success or failure of legitimisation can depend on this - even to the emergence of organised resistance groups.

If success legitimises itself, failure delegitimises itself – the longer the more. In this sense, the emergency poses few new questions, but accentuates familiar questions in a new and different way: a strong and efficient state with responsibly acting politicians is the best guarantee for successful legitimacy. A weak, underfunded, and under-equipped state may be sufficient under normal circumstances, but in an emergency becomes an overburdened state that brings about too little success and above all too little legitimacy.

If success legitimises itself, failure delegitimises itself – the longer the more. In this sense, the emergency poses few new questions, but accentuates familiar questions in a new and different way: a strong and efficient state with responsibly acting politicians is the best guarantee for successful legitimacy. A weak, underfunded, and under-equipped state may be sufficient under normal circumstances, but in an emergency becomes an overburdened state that brings about too little success and above all too little legitimacy.

4. Transgressing and Multiple Crises in Municipalities

4. 1 Ongoing administrative crisis?

For years, the financial shortage has been going on and is often coupled with over-indebtedness. This long-running situation is causing problems for many municipalities and is already severely restricting their ability to act, even without further crises. Although their ability to act is guaranteed by the right to municipalities to govern themselves pursuant to Article 28, Paragraph 2, Sentence 1 of the Basic Law, municipal government itself has been in crisis mode (un)indebted for decades (Hinkel, 1985, p. 225). The overburdening of municipalities leads primarily to less revenue on the one hand and more tasks in the course of decentralising tasks on the other (Grohs et al., 2012). This municipalisation is attractive due to its local relevance and as a legitimation resource: the top municipal administrations strive for more efficiency and proximity to the citizens when they execute tasks because they want to demonstrate success during their term of office so as not to jeopardise their re-election (Mehde, 2022). A tri-national study (including Germany) on the consequences of decentralisation positively shows both an increase in the horizontal coordination capacity on the ground and more effective task completion (Grohs et al., 2012). However, the additional financial costs have a negative impact on the municipal scope for action, "which regularly overburden weaker regional authorities in particular and can lead to deficits in implementation and ultimately to an increase in disparities. The municipalities' ways of reacting are [...] limited by too little fiscal leeway, so that municipalisations usually lead to shifts in the municipal task portfolio, which are at the expense of "voluntary" tasks" (Grohs et al., 2012, p. 143, German in original).

4. 2 Municipalities in crisis mode

In the past few years, municipalities coped with extraordinary tasks. In 2015 and 2016, shelter and care of over one million refugees posed a major challenge in terms of human, spatial and financial resources. From March 2020 until early April 2023, the measures to contain the Covid-19 pandemic led repeatedly to massive restrictions on fundamental rights for every individual and for many different sectors. The enormous negative impact of the pandemic manifests itself, among other things, in serious educational backlogs, especially among already lower-performing and disadvantaged students, and requires considerable social efforts in the long term. Since 24 February 2022, the war in Ukraine has superimposed the pandemic and is having cascading effects, which are reflected in a considerable increase in the number of refugees, especially from the Ukraine, inflation, energy insecurity, etc. The cursory enumeration of these crises illustrates their global and delimiting character (see also Schweizer's contribution in this volume). Although this global crisis mode affects all levels of the federal system, the municipalities have a special obligation. The municipalities must act locally because operational crisis management at the local level is predominantly in their hands and often catches them unprepared. With regard to the Covid-19 pandemic, this can be seen from a survey conducted by the opinion research institute Forsa on behalf of the magazine KOMMUNAL, in which 2,309 mayors in Germany participated in the initial phase of the pandemic (hereafter Ehrhardt, 2020). According to the survey, 75% of municipalities did not have contingency plans for an epidemic, which was particularly true for village communities (88%) and small towns (76%). In contrast, 79% of large cities had such plans. These plans proved to be useless because they were either outdated or related to other emergency situations (e.g., floods or major fires). The respondents had the following biggest problems in crisis managing at the beginning of the pandemic: maintaining the administration (21%), the financial or economic consequences (15%), the practical implementation of the measures (15%), and the control or compliance with the measures (10%). In the long term, they feared a significant loss of revenue (33%), economic losses (17%) and job losses (12%).

According to another study, these fears did not materialise despite pandemic-related losses (hereafter Boettcher & Freier, 2022). Compared to the banking crisis in 2009, when municipalities were plunged into a debt crisis, they are now in a better position and in many cases achieve slight financing surpluses, which is due on the one hand to more generous financial support from the federal and state governments and on the other hand to the resumption of revenues from municipal (business) taxes. However, the positive handling of the pandemic for the municipalities in fiscal terms is currently clouded by the ambiguous and uncertain development due to the aforementioned Russian attack on the Ukraine with its far-reaching consequences.

5. Crisis prevention

5. 1 Crisis management

Crisis management literature distinguishes between three temporal phases of crises: the pre-crisis as a phase of prevention and preparation, the acute crisis as a phase of coping, and the post-crisis as a phase of reflection and learning. Crisis prevention thus reflects only a part of the overall crisis work, which is presented as a cycle.

On the one hand, prevention can be understood as risk management. It can be used to anticipate and limit certain crisis triggers in advance – and thus, for instance, to counter the regular storm surges on the North Sea with improved dike construction. Risk management aims at avoiding crises. However, in view of the blurring of boundaries in today's crisis situations, it can only do part of the prevention work. Not only do cases such as the floods in the Ahr valley in Germany 2021 exceed common risk assumptions, but, as described, there are unpredictable social negotiations across different systems. Crisis prevention, on the other hand, must therefore mean being prepared for fundamental uncertainty. "Chaos phases" in crisis management can occur more often (in waves) or last longer – and should be prepared accordingly as "phases without a script". In addition to planning activities, a pre-crisis phase should moreover include preparations for dealing with uncertainty (lack of knowledge, vagueness of information and unpredictability). It should also be reflected that uncertainties can arise precisely because the population will be more actively involved than ever in negotiating crises.

Strengthening cooperation between organisations, sectors and knowledge domains can be an important aspect here. Relationship networks can be established in the pre-crisis phase to enable a rapid flow of information in the event of a crisis (cf. "High Reliability Networks (HRNs)", Berthod et al., 2016). This concerns, for example, the cooperation of emergency services and other stakeholders – but also that of decision-makers and experts. Different forms of knowledge must come together in order to cope with transgressing crises: Both specific expertise and abstract knowledge are required (cf. Brinks & Ibert, 2020). However, being able to relate expertise well to each other and to make both specific factual and process knowledge "viable" for decision-making is anything but trivial. Especially under the crisis-typical conditions of threat, urgency and uncertainty, pre-structured formats are needed. Moreover, knowledge is not simply "ready", but is created in the interaction between experts and decision-makers (cf. Berr et al., 2022). Expert opinions can differ or even contradict each other – and cause irritation among the population. Crisis prevention also means reflecting on these interrelationships and the difficulty of communicating them to the population in the pre-crisis period.

Considering prevention as part of the crisis management cycle means overall: accepting that crises will continue to occur. In this sense, quite independently of everyday business, it is a matter of building up a general understanding of crises as well as coping structures (e.g., emergency plans or task forces) in one's own organisation or authority. Likewise, the development of a good error culture can help to face the dynamics of the acute crisis.

5. 2 The importance of law

Law has no better forecasting or prevention capabilities than the other disciplines united here. However, this does not mean that it cannot make its own contribution to the issues discussed here. It is a matter of learning from the actual and legal findings of the crises that have taken place in the past and of better preparing the law for future emergencies.

What is needed is an effective professional and political evaluation of the events and experiences. They allow for conclusions to be drawn about strengths and weaknesses of existing law and thus specify the need for new or other regulations. For this purpose, expert knowledge must be consulted, as far as expert findings and statements are available. This may include scenarios being prepared for certain case groups, in part with parliamentary or ministerial support. Where expertise ends, political discussions are necessary. This applies, for example, to the process of prioritisation: Should emergency management resources be reduced during times without a disaster? In an emergency, it may then be too late. Conversely, what should get saved during times without emergencies in protection against major future losses everyone hopes will never occur? What about the political premium in this case particularly? Where is the legitimation regarding those at whom savings are now being made?

Lessons from a crisis must not be too concrete but must recognise preconditions and basic structures in a more abstract way. The next crisis does not have to be the same, it may be different. This is known where "scripts" have been drawn up. Incidentally, if you hoard respiratory masks after the pandemic, you may find that the next crisis is a flood where you would rather have needed rubber boots. The central issue lays not to in accumulating large quantities, but in opening up supply chains and logistics and in keeping them resilient.

Emergency management law must be appropriate regarding then target groups. This can justify differences between rules directed at enforcement staff and norms directed at potential victims or even everyone. The former may need to be alerted or at least informed earlier to be able to provide assistance. The latter should then be warned at the time and in such a way that no panic threatens to break out. Regarding panic in general: How people react under panic should be considered in legal cause-and-effect predictions.

Further discussion is also needed regarding the question of national peak and advisory boards to pool and assess information. The more established they are and the higher their standing is in the normal course of events, the more likely they are to be able to provide legitimacy in an emergency. Ideally, they can provide increased guidance for decision-makers, affected parties and the media, if they themselves are sufficiently legitimised.

5. 3 Crisis prevention in municipalities

In the pre-crisis phase, uncertainty prevails about the course and the outcome of the upcoming crisis. Municipalities must deal with this uncertainty and the resulting pressure. They make decisions to "get ahead of the situation" and avert the crisis, or to prepare for the acute phase and then manage it better. Under these conditions, bounded rationality can facilitate and improve decision-making. According to its originator, the psychologist and behavioural economist Herbert Simon, "bounded rationality" aims at decision-making under uncertainty by shortening and simplifying. For in crises "it is often necessary to proceed according to heuristic rules, to take 'mental shortcuts'. Such rules allow to prioritise some information and posteriorise others, to simplify complex decisions so that they are manageable, and to formulate measures that can be implemented quickly and without much delay, halfway thought through. These heuristic methods help to increase the probability of making a good decision, especially given the time and information constraints at hand" (Gómez Pomeri, 2022, pp. 87f., German in original).

In the acute crisis, already existing deficiencies in various areas of a municipality become apparent, which can intensify or grow more acute in the meantime. The Covid-19 pandemic exposed the already existing weaknesses in the health system in Germany regarding digitalisation as well as the consequences of economisation in nursing and care for the elderly. Even before the pandemic, the acute staff shortage was known as a nursing emergency (Özlü, 2020). The pandemic further worsened working conditions, consequently nursing staff either left the nursing sector or reduced their working hours. Although this trend continues, nursing and care for the elderly seem to compensate for the departures by hiring more new staff with higher salaries, thereby attempting to prevent crises at the same time (Beeger, 2022). A difficult undertaking for the municipalities also was implementing the rapidly changing measures to contain the virus during the acute phase of the pandemic, as crisis management demanded a great deal of flexibility and extra effort from staff over a long period of time: crisis teams met at weekends and on public holidays, administrative staff volunteered for crisis management or were delegated, they worked shifts and did overtime. However, due to the current accumulation of crises, municipalities do not return to the normal state of local government but remain in crisis mode and repeatedly reach the limits of their capacity (Erb, 2022).

Despite all the difficulties, German municipalities have largely succeeded in creating a flexible crisis prevention structure in recent years. In 2022, this learning process was evident when Ukrainian and other refugees were accommodated. However, with 1.2 million refugees within one year, municipalities were once again reaching their capacity limits (Dake, 2022). Two basic aspects manifest in dealing with refugees: firstly, communication with and participation of the population, and secondly, the development of a resilient municipality. Crisis communication sensitizes a large part of the population to counter the expected crisis-related loss of trust in the population, also within the local government and emergency services, and to provide behavioural norms along with information about the respective crisis (Schwarz et al., 2016). During a pandemic, the acceptance and adherence to norms of countermeasures to reduce the incidence of infection with its harmful to fatal consequences is also elementary. The need for compliance with rules is also conveyed by the police and municipal law enforcement services in personal dealings through fair and trust-building behaviour, which consolidates their perception of legitimacy among the population (Hecker, 2018).

The term "resilience" is currently in vogue. It originates from psychology and has recently been increasingly adopted in the social sciences. In sociology, it refers to the ability of societies to cope with external disturbances without sacrificing their important system functions (Blum et al., 2016).

At the local level, the direction of perspective is crucial for building resilience. For example, too much focus on the past can obscure the view of the future with its potential for innovation and learning (Endreß, 2022). In this sense, resilient communities are characterised by the fact that they "are able to shape themselves against the background of crisis experiences and thus possibly create new equilibria" (Endreß, 2022, p. 94, German in original). Building resilience requires a medium- and long-term perspective in dynamic and flexible municipalities in constant change.

6. Conclusion

"No crisis comes as a surprise; no crisis stands on its own, but is rather an interconnected phenomenon, typically with cascading effects" (Endreß, 2022, p. 93, German in original). Due to the ubiquity of the term crisis and the "multiple" occurrences of crisis cases, the contours of a crisis become blurred for science and practice. In addition, crises today typically occur without distinct boundaries. They cannot be clearly identified in terms of their often-global causes and consequences as they are the product of a complex social negotiation, often in an (inter)national context. As a result, municipalities are less concerned with negotiating crises than with their consequences and play an essential role in operational crisis management. In the federalist democracy of the Federal Republic of Germany, the constitutional guarantee of municipalities to govern themselves (Art. 28 (2) sent. 1 Basic Law) is of particular importance. However, additional legally obligatory duties and legally mandated matters by the federal and state governments considerably restrict the municipal scope for action if there is a lack of sufficient assumption of costs, especially in the case of financially weak municipalities.

Crises mean a legally exceptional state of affairs and create a special need for action. Therefore, the executive is primarily called upon in the acute situation. Crisis management includes prevention in three phases. Prevention is not only directed at avoiding crises, but also means dealing with uncertainty in a resilient manner by strengthening institutional networks and crisis communication with a population that participates and demands information. Before the crisis is after the crisis, and the post-crisis requires a professional and political evaluation of the events and experiences. Lessons from the crisis aim at both better crisis management and better adaptation of the law for future crises. Learning from crisis means recognising generalities from the mastered crisis with its preconditions and basic structures to be prepared for different, future crises.

Prolonged and repeatedly escalating crises prove to be a stress test for democracy. In view of the current accumulation of cases, municipalities can hardly get out of crisis mode, which makes structured and forward-looking crisis prevention more difficult. The local level also provides a stage for conflicts and protests by different groups ranging from anti-Covid-19 activists (so-called "Querdenker" in German) to climate activists. Municipalities must face up to the resulting challenges and ambivalences. They must endure and reflect on contradictions within the framework of the free democratic basic order. This democratic debate also promotes resilience in municipalities. Resilient municipalities see themselves as learning institutions open to alternatives. Consequently, they are supporting pillars of our federalist democracy, in which crises can also serve as turning points for fundamental reforms that improve the quality of life.

7. Literature

Ansell, C., Boin, A. & Keller, A. (2010). Managing transboundary crises: Identifying the building blocks of an effective response system. Journal of Contingencies and Crisis Management, 18(4), pp. 195-207.

Beeger, B. (2022). Trotz Pandemie steigt die Zahl der Pflegekräfte. (Despite pandemic, number of care-givers on the rise.) Frankfurter Allgemeine Zeitung. https://www.faz.net/aktuell/wirtschaft/mehr-wirtschaft/trotz-corona-pandemie-steigtdie-zahl-der-pflegekraefte-18019770.html.

Berthod, O., Grothe-Hammer, M., Müller-Seitz, G., Raab, J. & Sydow, J. (2016). From High-Reliability Organizations to High-Reliability Networks: The Dynamics of Network Governance in the Face of Emergency. Journal of Public Administration Research And Theory, 2017, pp. 352-371.

Boettcher, F., Freier, R. (2022). Zwei Jahre im Krisenmodus – die kommunalen Finanzen bleiben trotz-dem stabil. (Two years in crisis mode - municipal finances nevertheless remain stable.) Wirtschaftsdienst 102(8), pp. 6242-647.

Boin, A., t'Hart, P. & Kuipers, S. (2018). The Crisis Approach. In H. Rodriguez, E. Quarantelli & R. Dynes (Eds.), Handbook of Disaster Research (pp. 23-38). Springer.

Boin, A., Ekengren, M. & Rhinard, M. (2021). Understanding and Acting Upon a Creeping Crisis. In (Eds.), Understanding the Creeping Crisis (pp. 1-17). Palgrave Macmillan.

Bonß, W. (2021). Zwischen Normalisierung und Veränderung. (Between normalisation and change.) Zur Zukunft der zivilen Sicherheitsforschung. (On the future of civil security research.) In N. Eschenbruch, S. Kaufmann & P. Zoche (Eds.), Vielfältige Sicherheiten. (Multiple securities.) Gesellschaftliche Dimen-sionen der Sicherheitsforschung (Social Dimensions of Security Research.). Band 20 der Reihe: H.-J. Albrecht, R. Haverkamp, S. Kaufmann & P. Zoche (Eds.), Zivile Sicherheit (Civil Security): Schriften zum Fachdialog Sicherheitsforschung (pp. 37-55). LIT-Verlag.

Berr, K., Broer, I., Feldner, D., Harmsen, T., Schöppl, N., Sokolovska, N., Scherpenberg, C. V., Staemm-ler, J., Wagner, N., Walter, C. & Zoth, L. (2022). Der Crisis Science Hub: Krisenresilienz stärken durch systematische Zusammenarbeit von Wissenschaft und öffentlicher Verwaltung. (The Crisis Science Hub: Strengthening crisis resilience through systematic collaboration between science and public administration.) Institut für Innovation und Technik. https://www.iit-berlin.de/wp-content/uploads/2022/04/2022-03-28_iit-Studie-CRISP-Paper_final_Titel.pdf.

Blum, S., Endreß, M., Kaufmann, S. & Rampp, B. (2016). Soziologische Perspektiven. (Sociological per-spectives.) In R. Wink (Ed.), Multidisziplinäre Perspektiven der Resilienzforschung (Multidisciplinary perspectives on resilience research) (pp. 151-177). Springer.

Brinks, V. & Ibert, O. (2020). Krisenberatung: Sachliche und prozessuale Expertise in Krisen. (Crisis coun-selling: factual and procedural expertise in crises.) In F. Bösch, N. Deitelhoff & S. Kroll (Eds.), Hand-buch Krisenforschung (pp. 249-265). Springer.

Brinks, V. & Ibert, O. (2021). From omniscient narrator to involved participants: Places and spaces "acti-vated" in the EHEC O104:H4 crisis 2011. Journal of Contingencies and Crisis Management, 29(3), pp. 321-329.

Dake, B. (2022). Sind die Kommunen am Limit? (Are municipalities maxed out?) ARD-Tagesschau. https://www.tagesschau.de/inland/gesellschaft/fluechtlingszahlen-131.html.

Ehrhardt, C. (2020). Corona: Virus traf Deutschlands Kommunen unvorbereitet. (Corona: virus hit Ger-many's municipalities unprepared.) Kommunal. https://kommunal.de/corona-umfrage-buergermeister.

Endreß, M. (2022). Öffentliche Anhörung zur Definition und Erarbeitung eines Grundverständnisses des Begriffs „Krise" für die weitere Arbeit der Enquetekommission. Proceedings of the 3rd meeting of the committee of enquiry "Krisenfeste Gesellschaft" (Public hearing on the definition and development of a basic understanding of the term "crisis" for the further work of the Enquete Commission. Minutes of the 3rd meeting of the Enquete Commission "Crisis-proof Society"), public part, 24 June 2022, 17th Landtag Baden-Württemberg.

Erb, A. (2022). Kommunen im "Krisenmodus". (Municipalities in "crisis mode".) Der Neue Kämmerer. https://www.derneuekaemmerer.de/finanzen/nachhaltigkeit/kommunen-im-krisenmodus-21777/.

Gómez Pomeri, R. (2022). Die Corona-Zumutung. (The Corona Imposition.) Politik und Gesellschaft in Zeiten der Pandemie. (Politics and society in times of pandemic.) Springer.

Graf, Rüdiger (2020). Zwischen Handlungsmotivation und Ohnmachtserfahrung – Der Wandel des Kri-senbegriffs im 20. Jahrhundert. (Between motivation to act and experience of powerlessness - The transformation of the concept of crisis in the 20th century.) In F. Bösch, N. Deitelhoff & S. Kroll (Eds.), Handbuch Krisenforschung (Handbook of crisis research) (pp. 17-38). Springer.

Grohs, S., Bogumil, J. & Kuhlmann, S. (2012). Überforderung, Erosion oder Aufwertung der Kommunen in Europa? Eine Leistungsbilanz im westeuropäischen Vergleich. (Overstretch, erosion or upgrading of municipalities in Europe? A performance review in a Western European comparison.) der moderne staat - dms Zeitschrift für Public Policy, Recht und Management, 5(1), pp. 125-148.

Hecker, M. (2019). Vertrauen in die Stadt – Vertrauen in der Stadt. (Trust in the City - Trust within the City.) Die Wahrnehmungen polizeilicher Legitimität im städtischen Raum. (Perceptions of police legit-imacy in urban space.) LIT-Verlag.

Hinkel, K. R. (1985). Zur Situation der kommunalen Selbstverwaltung. (On the situation of local self-government.) Neue Zeitschrift für Verwaltungsrecht 4(4), pp. 225-230.

Homer-Dixon, T., Renn, O., Rockström, J., Donges, J.F. & Janzwood, S. (2022). A call for an internation-al research program on the risk of a global polycrisis. Technical Paper 2022-3, version 2.0. Cascade Institute. https://cascadeinstitute.org/technical-paper/a-

call-for-an-international-research-program-on-the-risk-of-a-global-polycrisis/.
Horn, E. (2014). Zukunft als Katastrophe. (Future as catastrophe.) S. Fischer Verlag.
Ibert, O. & Harmsen, T. (2022). Eingebettete Krisen: Bedrohung und Gelegenheit. (Embedded crises: Threat and opportunity.) Gesundheit + Gesellschaft Wissenschaft 3/22, pp. 7-14.
Jarren, O. & Neuberger, C. (Eds.) (2020): Gesellschaftliche Vermittlung in der Krise. (Social mediation in crisis.) Medien und Plattformen als Intermediäre. (Media and platforms as intermediaries.) Nomos.
Mehde, V. (2022). GG Art. 28 Abs. 2 GG. In R. Herzog, R. Scholz, M. Herdegen & H. H. Klein (Eds.), Dü-rig/Herzog/Scholz Grundgesetz-Kommentar (Rn. 1-179). C.H.Beck.
Nassehi, A. (2021). Unbehagen. (Discomfort.) Theorie der überforderten Gesellschaft. (Theory of the overstrained society.) C. H. Beck.
Özlü, I. (2020). Pandemie trifft Pflegenotstand. (Pandemic meets nursing emergency.) intensiv 28, pp. 122-125.
Preunkert, J. (2011). Die Krise in der Soziologie. (The crisis in sociology.) Soziologie, 40(4), pp. 432-442.
Roux-Dufort, C. (2007). Is Crisis Management (Only) a Management of Exceptions? Journal of Contin-gencies and Crisis Management, 15(2), pp. 105-114.
Schwarz, A., Schleicher, K., Srugies, A. & Rothenberger, L. (2016). Krise im Jugendamt. (Crisis in the Y-outh Welfare Office.) Leitfaden zur strategischen Krisenkommunikation für Kommunen. (Guide to strategic crisis communication for municipalities.) Köln: Nationales Zentrum Frühe Hilfen (NZFH).
Spector, B. (2019). There is no such thing as a crisis: A critique of and alterative to the dominant crisis management model. Journal of Contingencies and Crisis Management, 27(3), pp. 274-279.
Steg, J. (2020). Was heißt eigentlich Krise? (What does crisis actually mean?) Soziologie, 49(4), S. 423-435.
Voss, M. & Lorenz, D. F. (2016). Sociological Foundations of Crisis Communication. In A. Schwarz, M. W. Seeger & C. Auer (Eds.), The Handbook of International Crisis Communication Research 1, Wiley, pp. 45-55.

For further reading (in German)

Bösch, F., Deitelhoff, N. & Kroll, S. (Eds.). (2020). Handbuch Krisenforschung. (Handbook of crisis rese-arch.) Springer.

Kersten, J., Rixen, S. (2021). Der Verfassungsstaat in der Corona-Krise. (The constitutional state in the Corona crisis.) Schriftenreihe der Bundeszentrale für politische Bildung, Bd. 10626.

Papier, H. J., Behnke, N., Blom, A. G., Moser, E., El-Mafaalani, A., Biess, F., Ther, P. (2020). Corona-Krise. (Corona crisis.) Aus Politik und Zeitgeschichte (From Politics and Contemporary History), Heft 70, pp. 35-37.

Thießen, A. (Ed.). (2014). Handbuch Krisenmanagement. (Crisis management handbook.) Springer.

Media library (in German)

Podcast: Auch das noch?/Polykrise. Wie kommen wir da wieder raus? (That too?/Poly crisis. How do we get out of this?), Petra Pinzler und Stefan Schmitt auf ZEIT Online, 10.November.2022.

YouTube Video: Checkliste für den Fall der Fälle – Was müssen Kommunen im Katastrophen- und Zivilschutzfall machen? (Checklist for the worst-case scenario – What do municipalities have to do in the event of a disaster or civil protection?), Kanal: BehördenSpiegel, 08.April.2022.

YouTube Video Panel VII: Jetzt erst recht! Prävention in Zeiten von Krisen und Katastrophen (Now more than ever! Prevention in times of crises and disasters), panel discussion 27th DPT, 05.Oktober.2022.

Manuela Freiheit, Andreas Uhl and Andreas Zick

Crises and processing of crises

> *"In times of crisis, there is an increased risk of disinformation, conspiracy campaigns and transnational attacks on the free democratic basic order and its institutions."*

Our society is currently confronted with numerous conflicts and changes. The war in Ukraine, climate change and the Corona pandemic, growing social inequality and polarisation – the list of crises goes on and on. As research has shown, times of severe crisis are also times of extremism (cf. Klapsis, 2014). In times of crises, there is an increased risk of disinformation, conspiracy campaigns and transnational attacks on the free democratic basic order and its institutions. Simultaneously, group-focused enmity (Zick, Küpper & Heitmeyer, 2009) and radicalization phenomena are closely related to economic, social, and political conflicts, which can be experienced individually as insecurity and loss of control.

Especially in situations experienced as crises, radical and anti-democratic groups can seem attractive for people who are seeking for orientation, control, and a sense of belonging. According to the data published in the Munich Security Index 2022, it can be assumed that in crises such as the Corona pandemic, not only authoritarian regimes but also authoritarian and extremist groups gain in popularity as they are expected to provide security and the restoration of order and control (Bunde et al., 2023).

We therefore examine how societal groups deal with insecurity and uncertainty during crisis and conflict. How do they relate to radicalization processes and group-focused enmity? At the same time, there will be a focus on how insecurities are deliberately constructed and staged by populist and extremist groups and how they are used and instrumentalised for their own purposes. What does this mean for prevention, and what approaches and measures are available?

Conceptualisation of crises

When speaking of crisis events as drivers of group-focused enmity and authoritarian developments, it is first necessary to explain what generally characterises a crisis (cf. Koselleck, 1982; Mergel, 2012). However, research provides neither a generally accepted definition nor a universally valid understanding of the conditions, causes, processes and the impacts of crises. So far, it has not been possible to give a generally valid and binding answer to the question when an event or development can be classified as a crisis, when exactly a crisis is present, when it begins or ends, and how we can measure it empirically. Similarly, it is not possible to predict how crises will turn out and how crises will be evaluated afterwards (Steg, 2020, p. 429). Moreover, crises are always the subject of social and public debates. Through the inflationary use of crisis metaphors, the term also runs the risk of becoming an arbitrary and imprecise concept without any real significance (ibid.).

Another difficulty in defining crises lies in the dual structure of crisis indicators. Crises can be defined by objective factors, such as economic and financial crises. However, they always have a subjective dimension: they are perceived and interpreted, and this determines the extent of the perceived objective factors. The social philosopher Jürgen Habermas explicitly argues that one can only speak of crises "when members of a society experience structural alterations as critical for continued existence and feel their social identity threatened" (1988, p. 3); in other words, when members of society interpret and perceive a development as crisis-like. This makes it even more urgent to ask under what conditions crises occur, what determines their perception and at what point their consequences become visible (Koselleck & Richter, 2006).

Despite all the problems underlying the concept of crisis, it is possible to identify some central criteria that are characteristic of almost all types and forms of crises. In doing so, we do not claim to shed light on all aspects, but rather to highlight a few facets that are relevant in the context of the many current crises discussed in this article.

The sociologist Ulrich Oevermann (2016) has developed a concept for this perspective. According to this concept, crises are the culmination of events in which previous political, social, and economic procedures are no longer sufficient and effective. Thus, crisis events are largely beyond control and management (see also Frankenberg & Heitmeyer, 2022, p. 45; Steg, 2020, p. 430). Since their outcome is principally open, crises systematically produce a moment of ambiguity, uncertainty and refer to a future that cannot be assessed in advance. Secondly, the conditions before the crisis cannot be restored. Frankenberg and Heitmeyer (2022, p. 45) agree with this concept, but also emphasise that in crisis situations, which can neither be completely cognitively controlled nor preventively resolved, different ways of coping compete with each other. Among other things, this creates insecurity and uncertainty and, as currently observed, can fuel delusions and conspiracy myths (see e.g., Goertzel, 1994). The sociologist and philosopher Antonio Gramsci therefore also described crises as an "interregnum", an intermediate or transitional space in which the old perishes and the new cannot emerge (2011, p. 33). In this respect, crises and the analyses of crises always involve a struggle for hegemony, in which the aim is to assert a narrative and gain interpretive sovereignty over the crisis, i.e. the diagnosis of the crisis, the causes of the crisis and, in particular, the strategies for crisis management (Steg, 2020, p. 323).

In this regard, crises can also be determined by historical crisis phenomena. Looking at the last two decades, several crises can be identified:

- The terrorist attack on the World Trade Centre in New York on 11 September 2001 triggered a *religious-political* and *security crisis*.
- The passing of the Hartz IV laws in 2005 caused a *social crisis* for certain parts of the population, accompanied by considerable fears of social decline, which also spread to the middle class.
- After a short interval, the global banking and financial crisis of 2008-2009, as an *economic-political crisis*, put other parties under pressure and soon became a debt and (in Europe) a currency crisis.
- Finally, looking at the years 2015 and 2016, the migration of 1.5 million refugees to Germany needs to be mentioned, which has been perceived by some as an existential crisis. By politics and the media this was formatted as a *socio-cultural crisis* and perceived and portrayed by parts of the population as a social competition that threatens their very existence and the dominance of their own cultural identity (Heitmeyer, Freiheit & Sitzer, 2020, p. 45; see also Heitmeyer, 2018, pp. 91-93).

However, these crises were mitigated by the fact that they occurred over time and in different parts of society. In addition, there were different instruments available to contain these crises, at least to some extent (ibid.).

The *Corona pandemic* brought a new quality to the scene: in contrast to earlier crises, which affected subsystems and were then accompanied by specific losses of control of the affected groups and institutions, it was now losses of control of the health and the political regulatory systems that led to temporary closures or restrictions of areas of life and functional systems for all members of society (ibid.). Frankenberg and Heitmeyer's concept of crisis therefore distinguishes between two main types of crises: sectoral and systemic crises (Frankenberg & Heitmeyer, 2022, p. 46). While the first type focuses on crises affecting different spheres of life and functional systems of a society, the second type of crisis affects the social system as a whole. In addition to the *Corona/COVID-19* crisis, these also include, for example, the *climate crisis* and the *energy crisis* that has come to light since Vladimir Putin's war of aggression (ibid.).

Crisis events are processed differently, depending on individual affectedness and resilience, and translated differently into individual anxieties and collective fears. Nevertheless, "taken as a whole, they are likely to generate notions of loss of control and destabilization (Heitmeyer 2018, pp. 94-109), which can be identified as drivers of [group-focused enmity and] authoritarian aspirations" (Frankenberg & Heitmeyer, 2022, p. 45-46).

Crises have far-reaching consequences. They increase the likelihood of antidemocratic orientations by loss of control as well as threats, relative deprivations, authoritarian as well as dominance-oriented reactions that come with them. In the following chapter we want to explore this, and in particular show how crises and loss of control go hand in hand with hostile attitudes and radicalisation processes. In doing so, we pay particular attention to the results of representative population surveys in order to gain an impression of the social danger of crisis effects on the exclusion and devaluation of groups.

Crises as drivers of group enmity

It is well documented that the loss of control and the experience of threat as a result of perceived crisis favors devaluation processes of socially marked groups. For example, the attack on the World Trade Center on 11

September 2001 triggered fears of Islamist terrorism among many Americans. This resulted in an increase in hostility towards Islam and Muslims in American society (Goodwin & Devos, 2002; Pyszczynski, Solomon & Greenberg, 2003). Similar trends and attitudes can also be observed in Europe (see e.g. Bayrakli & Hafez, 2016; Pfeffer-Hoffmann & Fritsche, 2019). Theories on stereotypes and prejudice can explain why Islamist attacks have a high probability of increasing hostility towards Islam and Muslims: the attacks are associated with the group and social category of 'Muslims or Islam', and people who share this social category but are not involved in the attacks are attributed characteristics and blame for the attacks (Uenal et al., 2020). This 'scapegoat mechanism', which is consistently generated on political, media and social levels in society becomes obvious in crises when their causes remain unclear and 'outsiders' are blamed: "If there were no 'strangers', migration and immigrants, the crisis would not be so bad." Apart from massive violent events, this trend is commonly seen in times of economic and financial crises.

The study "Gruppenbezogene Menschenfeindlichkeit (GMF)" (Group-focused Enmity/GFE) published in the "Deutsche Zustände" (German Conditions) book series, has empirically shown this connection between the crisis years of 2008 and 2009 (cf. Heitmeyer, 2002-2012; Zick, Küpper & Heitmeyer, 2009). The data of the ten-year long-term study in Germany show that approval ratings for stereotypes and prejudices increased significantly due to simplistic crisis diagnoses from the middle of society. For example, Julia Becker and colleagues (2010) observed in their study that those who subjectively felt threatened by the economic and financial crisis tended to have more anti-Semitic and xenophobic attitudes than people who felt less affected. However, according to the authors' analysis the perceived threat of crises does not per se lead to more group-focused enmity. It is more important what or who is perceived as the cause of the crisis or to whom responsibility is attributed (Becker, Wagner & Christ, 2010, p. 138). People were more likely to agree with xenophobic statements if they suspected "foreigners" behind crises. If bankers and speculators were blamed, people who were subjectively affected by the crisis were more likely to hold anti-Semitic attitudes (ibid.). According to Becker, Wagner and Christ (2010), blame is attributed in particular to groups for which certain collective stereotypes and prejudices already existed (ibid., p. 140; also see Glick, 2002). Similar connections and causal attributions can also be found for the Corona crisis. For example, in the context of the various conspiracy myths, which in multiple variations connect to existing anti-Semitic attitudes in parts of the population and are picked up and mobilised by authoritarian and extremist groups (see also Heitmeyer, 2022, p. 263). In the face of fundamental social changes and insecurities, people may therefore tend to create scapegoats in order to find subjective explanations for social, political and economic distress (see also Billig, 1976; Tajfel, 1981; Glick, 2002).

Jürgen Mansel and Viktoria Spaiser (2010, p. 60) came to similar conclusions. They also show that the assessment of the economic and financial crisis is significantly linked to perceived control problems in relation to individual lifestyles, everyday life organization and life planning. And that corresponding experiences and fears are "favouring primarily the devaluation of such persons who are perceived as potential competitors for scarce goods" (ibid., p. 67).

Andreas Zick, Rebecca Lobitz and Eva Groß (2010) add another aspect to these interrelations. Not the individual feeling of being affected by the crisis, but the feeling of being a "crisis loser" leads to a crisis-related denouncement of equality and the devaluation and desolidarisation of socially weak groups (ibid., p. 83-84). This applies in particular to claims of establishment priviliges as well as to racist, xenophobic and Islamophobic resentments (ibid., p. 80). Similar results are documented in the cross-European GFE-Study (Zick, Küpper & Hövermann, 2011).

The German "Leipziger Autoritarismus-Studien" (Leipzig Authoritarianism Studies) came to similar conclusions. In the aftermath of the financial and economic crisis, they also observed a stronger rejection of migrants. Temporarily, these rejection values decreased significantly, but in recent years they have risen continuously again (Decker et al., 2022, p. 52). Also, in the "Bielefelder Mitte-Studie" (Bielefeld Middle Study) conducted in 2022/23, 26 per cent of the representative sample for Germany believed that too much consideration is given to minorities, and 34 per cent agreed that "in the national interest, we cannot grant everyone the same rights" (Zick, Küpper & Mokros, 2023).

Overall, the analyses indicate that the demonstrated patterns of prejudice that emerge during crises are not individual psychological dispositions. They are socially generated by groups, especially populist and extremist groups. They create enemy images of minorities especially in times of crisis. Thus, right-wing populist "leeways" and authoritarian temptations in times of crisis arise also depending on how people assess politicians' behaviour and their own lack of influence, and to what extent they are willing to engage themselves. For people who felt threatened, the assessments are and were much more negative. Also Control Theory approaches in social psychology (e.g., Lord & Levy, 1994) refer to the importance of control loss in the context of political and economic crises for the devaluation, discrimination and also violence against weak groups. Trust in democratic institutions can be considered as quite high in Germany (e.g., Küpper et al., 2021, p. 48). However, opposing this satisfaction with democracy, there is a continuously high level of political deprivation in both East and West Germany; i.e. a feeling of receiving less compared to others. It is about the discrepancy between a desired influence on politics and the perceived political powerlessness and lack of influence. In the 2020/2021 Middle Study, for instance, only 45 per cent of the respondents see possibilities of participating in their local environment. 28 per cent of the respondents also believe "people like me have no influence on what the government is doing anyway". The sentiment of political powerlessness is thereby lower than that of the 2018/2019 Middle Study, but overall only one in three respondents is convinced that they are able to influence government decisions (ibid., p. 49). More than one in five also doubts that a democracy can lead to appropriate decisions. 16 per cent of the respondents even think: "Our country is more like a dictatorship than a democracy now", a further 11 per cent of the respondents agree with this at least in part (Häusler & Küpper, 2021, p. 238).

Studies on right-wing populism also show that people subjectively affected by crises have significantly higher approval values for right-wing populist attitudes than those subjectively not affected (cf. Schaefer, Mansel & Heitmeyer, 2002; Zick, Küpper & Mokros, 2023; Metten & Bayerlein, 2023). The anomie linked with crises or the perception of a lack of rules can make people receptive to populism and extremism (cf. Hövermann, Messner & Zick, 2015). Particularly during times that are perceived as complicated, confusing, contradictory and unsettling, there is an increased likelihood of finding claims of simple truths and solutions or good-and-evil schemes of authoritarian and extremist ideologies appealing. Similarly, the number of organised groups and movements that are promising solutions and salvation increases, as witnessed during the corona pandemic (e.g., Heinze & Weisskircher, 2022). It is therefore even more relevant to understand how people deal with this affective side effects such as fear, uncertainty or powerlessness that crises inevitably bring with them.

Processing and instrumentalisation of crises

The fact that people have a basic need for control and self-efficacy is well documented in research. Unexpected events and crises can disrupt this image of a secure understanding of the social environment (Hogg et al., 2007) and an autonomous self, and thus create feelings of uncertainty, powerlessness and helplessness (Zick & Sandal-Önal, 2023). Stress theoretical approaches (e.g. Lazarus & Laier, 1981) conclude that situations perceived as uncontrollable affect the self-esteem as they are interpreted as weakness in introspection, especially in a system which is oriented towards performance and a demonstration of strength. Therefore, it is quite natural that people pursue different processing and coping strategies to compensate for the loss of personal control and to counter the feeling of helplessness towards crises. For example, "immunisations" can be used that propagate a "carry on" despite ongoing crises (Heitmeyer, Freiheit & Sitzer, 2020, p. 46). Consistently, studies show a splitting or fragmentation of reality due to different assessments of the social and the individual situation: "Society is doing poorly, but I (and my personal environment) are doing well" (ibid.).

Believing in conspiracy myths (Whitson & Galinsky, 2008), esoteric ideologies and collective blaming are further compensation and processing strategies. They can be directed against "those up there", but also against "those down there" as well as other social groups (Wodak, KhosraviNik & Mral, 2013). By attributing blame or power and a capacity for action to certain actors, the image of an orderly and explainable world shall be straightened out.

Such defensive reactions and causal attributions are not unique to individuals. Groups can also pursue them collectively and thus develop and strengthen radical ideologies. Moreover, defending against the experience of powerlessness and the shared need for control and ability to act can also be achieved through a collective denial of the situation (e.g., Sandrin, 2021). Examples for this are the denial of the climate crisis or statements like "there is no pandemic". In addition, in terms of Social Identity Theory (Tajfel & Turner, 1986) devaluing weak groups can serve the function of revaluing a damaged self that was affected by the sense of loss of control. People strengthen their sense of belonging, unity and collective efficacy by complying with the predominant beliefs of their in-group. Therefore, people's belief in being a part of an efficient and closely-knit group compensates for the loss of control (ibid.).

Furthermore, norms of solidarity can be revoked and establishment privileges can be claimed ("Us first"; "Germans first") as well as trust in democratically legitimised politics can be withdrawn (Heitmeyer, 2018, pp. 105-106; Heitmeyer, Freiheit & Sitzer, 2020, p. 46). This pattern is often associated with political apathy and a possible retreat from the community as a result (ibid.). Finally, because of the permanent stress of crises and the constant threat of losing control, a longing for reassurance and the restoration of order may also emerge. This can lead to various political demands, such as the control of banks and corporations, or political decisions that are supposedly directed against "the people", or even for a more rigid refugee policy (Heitmeyer, 2018, p. 106).

Some of these processing and compensation strategies are more receptive to anti-democratic and authoritarian offerings than others. According to Need Theories, radicalisation occurs particularly when individuals can't see a way to meet their basic psychological needs as individuals or as members of socially accepted, non-radical groups (e.g. Correll & Park, 2005). It should be emphasised, however, that these processes do not even require the presence of an actual threat to basic needs. The subjective perception of a threat alone can lead people to turn increasingly towards their own groups (cf. e.g. Thomas & Thomas, 1928; Stephan et al., 2016).

There lie considerable dangers in this. As demontrated, people may react with simplified worldviews or stereotypes in order to regain order, structure, and control when situations or the presence of people are perceived as unpredictable or uncontrollable.

Authoritarian and extremist groups in particular know how to exploit these orientation patterns. This has already been well described in Leo Löwenthal and Norbert Gutermann's study of agitation in American fascism (Löwenthal & Gutermann, 2021). By pointing out and denouncing unequal treatment and grievances or creating dark scenarios for the future, extremist propagandists create a strong sense of threat in people, which they exaggerate even further in their agitation and therefore creating massive feelings of powerlessness. At the same time, they present and portray themselves as saviours in times of need, i.e. they have the (apparently) appropriate solution at hand to counteract any threat. However, authoritarian and extremist groups do not only draw on already existing attitudes and stereotypes in society or exploit feelings of fear and insecurity. They also deliberately use unsettling information to create a maximum of uncertainty, putting people and groups in a state of loss of control and leading them to change their attitudes.

In our view, modern digital worlds in social media have become significantly important and accelerated these dynamics. As many aspects of life shifted to digital realms during the height of the corona pandemic in part due to containment measures, false reports could reach a lot of people much more easily making it easier for uncertainties to catch on. The utilization of uncertainty is therefore a central mode for understanding polarisation and recognising how social groups can use uncertainties to create and shape conflicts.

Given these developments, it is understandable that teaching tolerance for ambiguity and ambivalence can be seen as a fundamental goal of pedagogical and social work. It is also seen as a "central task of civic education" (Bothe, 2020, p. 75) and prevention. Especially adolescents and young people should be strengthened in their individual resilience enabling them to contrast different and opposing perspectives and positions, tolerate contradictions, and develop their own judgements and ideas about how to live together in society (Müller, 2021, p. 59). In principle, the promotion of resilience can be directed at individuals, but also address larger groups or entire societies (see also Dreßing, 2023, pp. 64-66).

In the concluding chapter, we will therefore take a closer look at what role tolerance of ambiguity and ambivalence can play in educational work and prevention which among other things aims to prevent polarisation, radicalisation and ideologisation and to promote democratic values (see also Müller, 2021, p. 58).

Implications for prevention

Modern societies create many ambiguities (e.g. Beck, 1983; Bauman, 1993), while clarity and unambiguousness seem to have been irretrievably lost in the course of this development. For this reason alone, the ability to tolerate ambiguity and ambivalence, i.e. to endure ambiguous, sometimes even contradictory situations in the modern world would be particularly important, if not necessary (including Frenkel-Brunswick, 1949; Krappmann, 1969; Reis, 1997; Stangl, 2021).

However, Thomas Bauer (2018) has shown that the tolerance of ambiguity in particular is constantly declining and he pointed to fatal consequences for society and politics. Following Bauer's thesis that "our time is a time of low tolerance of ambiguity", it is easy to understand why especially those offers appear attractive to people that promise "a redemption from the inescapable ambiguity of the world" (ibid., p. 30). Accordingly, diversity and plurality are no longer perceived as enriching but as burdensome (ibid.).

Blurred social coordinates also make it difficult to reassure and locate one's own and other's positions in social space: Is someone on the political left or on the right, is someone socio-economically at the "top" or "bottom"? Is someone in an ethnoculturally open or closed society? Is this society socio-culturally homogeneous or heterogeneous? What is true or false in the face of so-called fake news and disinformation? This blurring can activate search movements for political actors who pretend to resolve such contradictions, turning ambiguities into apparent clarities and promising the restoration of control (Heitmeyer, 2018, pp. 109-112; Heitmeyer, 2022, pp. 258-259).

Claudia Lenz therefore describes tolerance of ambiguity not only as an individual "ability to deal constructively with inconclusiveness and uncertainty", but as a "quality which is crucial for the democratic functioning of pluralistic and diverse societies" (Lenz, 2021, p. 3). Besand even calls this the "central civic virtue" of a democracy (Besand, 2021, p. 244) in dealing with social diversity and contradictions. Tolerance of ambiguity is also not limited to tolerating perspectives, opinions, positions, attitudes and values that differ from one's own. Tolerance of ambiguity means being able to endure fundamentally contradictory positions and opinions, as well as the knowledge that "there are in fact no ultimate justifications" and that "everything we say [can] turn out to be wrong in the long run". (Besand, 2021, p. 245). It is about "a largely mutual recognition in difference", which can also be described as "difference compatibility", whereby different beliefs, perspectives and interpretations can stand side by side equally, i.e. in coexistence (Saner, 2013). This includes the "recognition of divergent points of view, interests and arguments", also the "willingness to change one's own standpoints [...] and patterns of interpretation", as well as the "acknowledgement of differences as being of equal value" and the "appreciation of non-understanding as a starting point for new insight" (Lenz, 2021, p. 4).

Strengthening tolerance of ambiguity and ambivalence is hence a comprehensive task for society as a whole. It cannot be carried out by one target group alone, such as adolescents or young people, but requires the involvement of all. In the case of schools, for example, this would include not only the students but also primarily the pedagogical staff, "who must be able to deal with ambiguity, pluralism and differences or be diversity-sensitive to prevent polarisation and ideologisation in order for participation and inclusion to succeed" (Müller, 2021, p. 61).

In prevention, various formats can be used in order to achieve these goals. According to Müller (2021, p. 65), dilemma training and biographical work are particularly suitable for "practising the change of perspective as well as the recognition and endurance of contradictions, uncertainties and fears". In general, formats that include a change of perspective are key to the development of tolerance for ambiguity and ambivalence. Different points of view should always be allowed in order to show complexities in different realities of life. It is also important not to lecture or give one perspective more importance than another. Through open discourse positive behaviour is encouraged and reinforced, at the same time boundaries should be shown when discussions become offensive or hurtful (Danner et al., 2021, p. 13). Truth claims should also be analysed and questioned without determining questions of guilt (e.g. on the topic of the Middle East conflict). The focus should also not lie on avoiding problematic behaviour or extremist attitudes (ibid.) but on giving space to thought patterns and arguments rather than stiffening solely on ideological standpoints (ibid.).

According to Kiehl and Schnerch, allowing and recognising other opinions and perspectives is also a central democratic competence (2018, p. 116). School is one of the places where tolerance of ambiguity and ambivalence can be developed. So, it is not surprising that schools are the focus of many prevention efforts, especially since young people are one of the main target groups for prevention programs in Germany (see Lützinger et al., 2020, p. 604).

For a better understanding to which extent formats for promoting tolerance of ambiguity and ambivalence are already carried out in schools, data from the MAPEX research project can be used as a reference.[1] Out of the 423 projects and measures in the MAPEX data set that are focusing on the field of action of schools, 97 per cent (n = 412) aim at promoting tolerance and appreciation. At the same time, only 4 per cent (n = 16) of these offerings address empowerment and the strengthening of resilience as the intention of their projects.[2] This indicates that there are needs and gaps that have not been fully addressed, yet. When it comes to strengthening resilience and empowerment mainly educational formats are used. But also formats of intercultural exchange, sport, music and theatre are used in this context. In research these different formats appear promising for the training of tolerance of ambiguity and ambivalence. Especially various areas of the arts which are generally characterised by ambiguity can be helpful. According to Kiehl and Schnerch (2018, p. 118), "[here] lie approaches to practising maturity and dealing with contradictions".

Choosing school as an example also clearly demonstrates the primary focus of prevention efforts in Germany, also when it comes to developing tolerance of ambiguity and ambivalence. Based on the MAPEX data, additional gaps in the prevention landscape can be identified here. For example, across all 588 offered formats in the MAPEX data set, only about one third of these offers (32 per cent; n = 186) address adults as a target group. Nineteen per cent (n = 111) are directed at professionals[3] in the field of action of schools. Of these, 98 per cent (n = 109) aim to promote tolerance and respect while 8 per cent (n = 9) aim at empowerment and strengthening of resilience. Offers that explicitly promote resilience among parents and/or relatives of radicalised or vulnerable persons, on

1 While the MAPEX data was collected with a focus on Islamist radicalisation, there are also numerous cross-phenomena and non-phenomena-specific perspectives included. See also www.mapex-projekt.de.

2 For this purpose, the filter "School" was selected in the category "Fields of action" in the MAPEX platform.

3 In this case, the filter "School" was selected in the MAPEX platform's category "Fields of action", the filter "Professionals, multipliers, etc." in the category "Target group" and "Adults (from 27)" in the category "Addressed age groups".

the other hand, only appear twice in the data set. Consequently, additional programs are needed to strengthen the tolerance for ambiguity and ambivalence of professionals working in schools, as well as of parents and relatives. And they should also be more included in prevention efforts. A stronger focus on these target groups, also within the framework of federal and state prevention programs, could have a supporting effect here.

As mentioned at the beginning, it is not only up to pupils and young people as well as their parents and school professionals to develop resilience in dealing with ambivalences and ambiguities. Other target groups and society itself must also be brought into focus in order to prevent polarisation and ideologisation and help participation and inclusion succeed. As resilience research shows, the promotion of individual resilience is interrelated with societal resilience (e.g. Fathi, 2019 and 2020), as the former positively influences the latter. With Gilan and Helmreich, individual resilience can thus also be understood as the basis for societal crisis management (see Gilan & Helmreich, 2023, p. 79).

In order to be able to reach people on a broad level adequately, the necessary structural framework has to be created. In part, projects and measures with broad target groups can already be found in currently funded projects. For example, the National Action Plan against right-wing extremism by the German government includes targeted support for a culture of democratic debate to strengthen the ability to manage conflicts and engage in dialogue to prevent polarization, division and disinformation.[4] Such projects could be a building block to give ambiguities a space in society, while also learning to tolerate them better. And thereby support a change of perspective that focuses on commonalities without equalizing differences. Adapting a Willy Brandt slogan from 1969, Müller suggests that "Dare more ambiguity" could be a possible conclusion (2021, p. 67). Because a different culture of discourse and discussion, as Müller puts it, "could have an inclusive and also - quite incidentally - a preventive effect. In the classroom and in public space" (ibid.).

4 The program "MITEINANDER REDEN" (Talking To Each Other) initiated by the Federal Agency for Civic Education in Germany is explicitly mentioned here. Participatory dialogs and appreciative negotiation processes should contribute to the strengthening of a democratic political culture in order to meet the challenges of a polarising society for "new forms of social interaction, dialog, resilience as well as decision-making and responsibility" (Bundeszentrale für politische Bildung, 2023).

Literature

Bauer, T. (2018). Die Vereindeutigung der Welt. Über den Verlust an Mehrdeutigkeit und Vielfalt. Reclam.

Bauman, Z. (1993). Modernity and Ambivalence. Polity Press.

Bayrakli, E. & Hafez, F. (2016). The state of Islamophobia in Europe. European Islamophobia Report, pp. 5-11.

Beck, U. (1983). Jenseits von Stand und Klasse? Soziale Ungleichheit, gesellschaftliche Individualisierungsprozesse und die Entstehung neuer Formationen und Identitäten. In R. Kreckel (Ed.), Soziale Ungleichheiten, Soziale Welt, Sonderband 2 (pp. 35-74).

Becker, J., Wagner, U. & Christ, O. (2010). Ursachenzuschreibungen in Krisenzeiten: Auswirkungen auf Antisemitismus und Fremdenfeindlichkeit. In W. Heitmeyer (Ed.), Deutsche Zustände. Folge 8 (pp. 128-143). Suhrkamp.

Besand, A. (2021). Was Ambiguitätstoleranz (möglicherweise) nicht ist. In A. Schnurr, S. Dengel, J. Hagenberg & L. Kelch (Eds.), Mehrdeutigkeit gestalten: Ambiguität und die Bildung demokratischer Haltungen in Kunst und Pädagogik (pp. 241-251). Transcript.

Billig, M. (1976). Social Psychology and Intergroup Relations. Academic Press.

Bothe, L. (2020). Ambiguitätstoleranz als Ausgangspunkt für die Praxis der politischen Bildung. In Gegen Vergessen – für Demokratie e. V. (Eds.): Konstruktive Kommunikation in der Demokratie. Ein Baustein in der politischen Bildung (pp. 70-79). https://www.gegen-vergessen.de/fileadmin/user_upload/Gegen_Vergessen/Dokumente/Broschueren/konstruktive-Kommunikation_2020-web.pdf. Retrieved March 19, 2023.

Bunde, T., Eisentraut, S., Knapp, N., Schütte, L., Hammelehle, J., Kump, I., Mudie-Mantz A. & Pauly, J. (2023). Munich Security Report 2023: Re:vision. MSC: Munich Security Conference.

Bundeszentrale für politische Bildung (Eds.). (2023). https://miteinander-reden.net/foerderprogramm/ziele/. Retrieved March 27, 2023.

Correll, J. & Park, B. (2005). A model of the ingroup as a social resource. Personality and Social Psychology Review, 9(4), pp. 341-359.

Danner, K., Hofinger, V. & Walter, R. (2021). Good Practices der Extremismusprävention im Bildungsbereich, IRKS Working Paper Nr. 21. https://www.beratungsstelleextremismus.at/wpcontent/uploads/2021/06/WorkingPaper26_5_2021.pdf. Retrieved March 19, 2023.

Decker, O., Kiess, J., Heller, A. & Brähler, E. (2022). Autoritäre Dynamiken in unsicheren Zeiten: Neue Herausforderungen – alte Reaktionen? In O. Decker, J. Kiess, A. Heller & E. Brähler (Eds.), Autoritäre Dynamiken in unsicheren Zeiten: Neue Herausforderungen – alte Reaktionen? (pp. 11-28). Psychosozial-Verlag.

Dreßing, H. (2023). Die Bedeutung psychischer Resilienz im Zusammenhang mit Krisen. In G. R. Wollinger, C. Heizelmann & E. Marks (Eds.), Krisen & Prävention. Expertisen zum 28. Deutschen Präventionstag (pp. 57 71). Forum Verlag Godesberg GmbH.

Fathi, K. (2019). Resilienz im Spannungsfeld zwischen Entwicklung und Nachhaltigkeit: Anforderungen an gesellschaftliche Zukunftssicherung im 21. Jahrhundert. https://doi.org/10.1007/978-3-658-26941-8. Retrieved March 22, 2023.

Fathi, K. (2020). Die multi-resiliente Gesellschaft: Orientierungspunkte für die Corona-Krise und darüber hinaus. Forschungsjournal Soziale Bewegungen, 33, 22-36. https://doi.org/10.1515/fjsb-2020-0004. Retrieved March 22, 2023.

Frankenberg, G. & Heitmeyer, W. (2022). Autoritäre Entwicklungen. Bedrohungen pluralistischer Gesellschaften und moderner Demokratien in Zeiten der Krisen. In G. Frankenberg & W. Heitmeyer (Eds.), Treiber des Autoritären. Pfade von Entwicklungen zu Beginn des 21. Jahrhunderts (pp. 15-86). Campus.

Frenkel-Brunswick, E. (1949). Intolerance of Ambiguity as an Emotional and Perceptional Personality Variable. Journal of Personality, 18/1949, pp. 108-143.

Gilan, D. & Helmreich, I. (2023). Die resiliente Gesellschaft – eine kollektive Antwort auf kollektive Probleme. In G. R. Wollinger, C. Heizelmann & E. Marks (Eds.), Krisen & Prävention. Expertisen zum 28. Deutschen Präventionstag (pp. 73-89). Forum Verlag Godesberg GmbH.

Glick, P. (2002). Sacrifical lambs dressed in wolves' clothing: Envious prejudice, ideology, and the scapegoating of jews. In L.S. Newman & R. Erber (Eds.), Understanding genocide: The social psychology of the Holocaust (pp. 113-142). Oxford University Press.

Goertzel, T. (1994). Belief in conspiracy theories. In Political Psychology (Vol. 15, Issue 4, p. 731).

Goodwin, S. & Devos, T. (2002). American Identity Under Siege: National and Racial Identities in the Wake of the September 11th Attack. Vortrag auf der Jahrestagung der Society for Experimental Social Psychology.

Gramsci, A. (2011). Prison Notebooks. Vereinigtes Königreich: Columbia University Press.

Habermas, J. (1988). Legitimation Crisis. Polity Press.

Häusler, A. & Küpper, B. (2021). Rechtsextreme Widerstandspostulate und völkisch autoritäre Rebellion. In A. Zick & B. Küpper (Eds.): Die geforderte Mitte. Rechtsextreme und demokratiegefährdende Einstellungen in Deutschland 2020/2021 (pp. 225-261). Dietz.

Heinze, A.-S. & Weisskircher, M. (2022). How Political Parties Respond to Pariah Street Protest: The Case of Anti-Corona Mobilisation in Germany. In German Politics (Vol. 32, Issue 3, pp. 563–584). Informa UK Limited.

Heitmeyer, W. (Ed.) (2002-2012). Deutsche Zustände. Folge 1-10. Suhrkamp.

Heitmeyer, W. (2018). Autoritäre Versuchungen. Suhrkamp.

Heitmeyer, W., Freiheit, M. & Sitzer, P. (2020). Rechte Bedrohungsallianzen. Suhrkamp.

Heitmeyer, W. (2022). Krisen und Kontrollverluste – Gelegenheitsstrukturen für Treiber autoritärer gesellschaftlicher Entwicklungspfade. In G. Frankenberg & W. Heitmeyer (Eds.), Treiber des Autoritären. Pfade von Entwicklungen zu Beginn des 21. Jahrhunderts (pp. 251-280). Campus.

Hogg, M. A., Sherman, D. K., Dierselhuis, J., Maitner, A. T. & Moffitt, G. (2007). Uncertainty, entitativity, and group identification. Journal of Experimental Social Psychology, 43, pp. 135-142.

Hövermann, A., Messner, S. F. & Zick, A. (2015). Anomie, marketization, and prejudice toward purportedly unprofitable groups: Elaborating a theoretical approach on anomie-driven prejudices. Acta Sociologica, 58(3), pp. 215-231.

Kiehl, C. & Schnerch, B. (2018). Demokratiekompetenzen auf dem Prüfstand – Schule als Erfahrungsraum für Mündigkeit und Ambiguitätstoleranz? https://www.idz-jena.de/fileadmin/user_upload/PDFS_WsD3/Text_Kiehl_Schnerch.pdf. Retrieved March 22, 2023.

Klapsis, A. (2014). Economic Crisis and Political Extremism in Europe: From the 1930s to the Present. In European View (Vol. 13, Issue 2, pp. 189–198). SAGE Publications.

Koselleck, R. (1982): Krise. In O. Brunner, W. Conze & R. Koselleck (Eds.), Geschichtliche Grundbegriffe. Historisches Lexikon zur politisch-sozialen Sprache in Deutschland. Band 3 (pp. 617-650). Klett-Cotta.

Koselleck, R. & Richter, M. W. (2006). Crisis. Journal of the History of Ideas, 67(2), 357–400.

Krappmann, L. (1969). Soziologische Dimensionen der Identität. Strukturelle Bedingungen für Teilnahme an Interaktionsprozessen. Klett-Cotta.

Küpper, S., Berghan, W., Zick, A. & Rump, M. (2021). Volkes Stimme – antidemokratische und populistische Einstellungen. In A. Zick & B.

Küpper (Eds.): Die geforderte Mitte. Rechtsextreme und demokratiegefährdende Einstellungen in Deutschland 2020/2021 (pp. 43-74). Dietz.

Lazarus, R.S. & Lannier, R. (1981). Streßbezogene Transaktionen zwischen Person und Umwelt. In J. R. Nitsch (Ed.), Streß. Theorien, Untersuchungen, Maßnahmen (pp. 231-258). Hogrefe AG.

Lenz, C. (2021). Ambiguitätstoleranz: Ein zentrales Konzept für Demokratiebildung in diversen Gesellschaften. https://www.ufuq.de/aktuelles/ambiguitaetstoleranz-ein-zentrales-konzeptfuer-demokratiebildung-in-diversen-gesellschaften/. Retrieved March 22, 2023.

Lord, R. G. & Levy, P. E. (1994). Moving from Cognition to Action: A Control Theory Perspective. In Applied Psychology (Vol. 43, Issue 3, pp. 335–367). Wiley.

Löwenthal, L. & Guterman, N. (2021). Prophets of Deceit: A Study of the Techniques of the American Agitator. Verso Books.

Lützinger, S., Gruber, F. & Hedayat, A. (2020). Eine Bestandsaufnahme präventiver Angebote in Deutschland sowie ausgewählter Präventionsstrategien aus dem europäischen Ausland. In B. Ben Slama & U. Kemmesies (Eds.), Handbuch Extremismusprävention: Gesamtgesellschaftlich. Phänomenübergreifend (pp. 597-626). Bundeskriminalamt.

Mansel, J. & Spaiser, V. (2010). Ängste und Kontrollverlust. Zusammenhänge mit Gurppenbezogener Menschenfeindlichkeit. In W. Heitmeyer (Ed.), Deutsche Zustände. Folge 8 (pp. 49-71). Suhrkamp.

MAPEX-Forschungsverbund (Eds.). (2021). MAPEX-Plattform. https://www.mapex-projekt.de/datenvisualisierung/. Retrieved March 20, 2023.

Metten, A. & Bayerlein, M. (2023). Existential anxieties and right-wing populism in Europe – why people unconcerned by globalisation vote against it. In Zeitschrift für Vergleichende Politikwissenschaft (Vol. 17, Issue 1, pp. 1–30). Springer Science and Business Media LLC.

Mergel, 2012 (Ed.). (2012). Krisen verstehen. Historische und kulturwissenschaftliche Annäherungen. Campus.

Müller, J. (2021). Recht behalten ist auch keine Lösung. Ambiguitätstoleranz in der Islamismusprävention. In Kompetenznetzwerk „Islamistischer Extremismus" (KN:IX) (Eds.), Herausforderungen, Bedarfe und Trends im Themenfeld. Report 2021 (pp. 58-67). Violence Prevention Network gGmbH.

Oevermann, U. (2016). „Krise und Routine" als analytisches Paradigma in den Sozialwissenschaften. In R. Becker-Lenz, A. Franzmann,

Axel Jansen & M. Jung (Eds.), Die Methodenschule der Objektiven Hermeneutik. Eine Bestandsaufnahme (pp. 43-114). Springer VS.

Pfeffer-Hoffmann, C. & Fritsche, C. (Eds.) (2019). Muslimfeindlichkeit in Europa. Umgang mit einem Alltagsphänomen. Mensch & Buch.

Pyszczynski, T., Solomon, S. & Greenberg, J. (2003). In the Wake of 9/11: The Psychology of Terror. American Psychological Association.

Reis, J. (1997). Ambiguitätstoleranz. Beiträge zur Entwicklung eines Persönlichkeitskonstrukts. Asanger.

Sandrin, P. (2021). The Rise of Right-Wing Populism in Europe: A Psychoanalytical Contribution. In Financial Crisis Management and Democracy (pp. 227–239). Springer International Publishing.

Saner, H. (2013). Von der Toleranz zur Differenzverträglichkeit. Aktuelle juristische Praxis, 309, pp. 31-43.

Schaefer, D., Mansel, J. & Heitmeyer, W. (2002). Rechtspopulistisches Potential. Die „saubere Mitte" als Problem. In W. Heitmeyer (Ed.), Deutsche Zustände. Folge 1 (pp. 123-144). Suhrkamp.

Stangl, W. (2021). Stichwort „Ambiguitätstoleranz". Online Lexikon für Psychologie und Pädagogik. https://lexikon.stangl.eu/12220/ambiguitaetstoleranz/. Retrieved March 22, 2023.

Steg, J. (2020). Was heißt eigentlich Krise? Soziologie, 49(4), pp. 423-435.

Stephan, W. G., Ybarra, O. & Rios, K. (2016). Intergroup threat theory. In T. D. Nelson (Ed.), Handbook of prejudice, stereotyping, and discrimination (pp. 255-278). Psychology Press.

Tajfel, H. (1981). Human Groups and Social Categories: Studies in Social Psychology. Cambridge University Press.

Tajfel, H. & Turner, J. C. (1986). The social identity theory of intergroup behavior. In S. Worchel & W. G. Austin (Eds.), Psychology of intergroup relations (pp. 7–24). Nelson-Hall.

Thomas, W. I., Thomas, D. S. (1928). The Child in America: Behavior Problems and Programs. Knopf.

Uenal, F., Bergh, R., Sidanius, J., Zick, A., Kimel, S. & Kunst, J. R. (2020). The Nature of Islamophobia: A Test of a Tripartite View in Five Countries. In Personality and Social Psychology Bulletin (Vol. 47, Issue 2, pp. 275–292). SAGE Publications.

Whitson, J. A. & Galinsky, A. D. (2008). Lacking Control Increases Illusory Pattern Perception. Science, 322 (5898), pp. 115-117.

Wodak, R., KhosraviNik, M. & Mral, B. (Eds.). (2013). Right-Wing Populism in Europe. Bloomsbury Publishing Plc.

Zick, A., Küpper, B. & Heitmeyer, W. (2009). Prejudices and group-focused enmity: a socio-functional perspective. In A. Pelinka, K. Bischof & K. Stögner (Eds.), Handbook of Prejudice (pp. 273-303).

Cambria Press.
Zick, A., Lobitz, R. & Groß, E. (2010). Krisenbedingte Kündigung der Gleichwertigkeit. In W. Heitmeyer (Ed.), Deutsche Zustände. Folge 8 (pp. 72-86). Suhrkamp.
Zick, A., Küpper, B. & Hövermann, A. (2011). Intolerance, Prejudice and Discrimination - A European Report. Berlin: Friedrich-Ebert-Stiftung.
Zick, A., Küpper, B. & Mokros, N. (Eds.). (2023). Die distanzierte Mitte: Rechtsextreme und demokratiegefährdende Einstellungen in Deutschland 2022/23 (ed. for the Friedrich-Ebert-Stiftung, Fr. Schröter). Dietz.
Zick, A. & Sandal-Önal, E. (2023). Uncertainty in Conflicts between Societal Groups – A Social Psychological View (Center for Uncertainty Studies Working Papers, 4). Universität Bielefeld, Center for Uncertainty Studies (CeUS).

For further reading

Diamond, J. (2019). Upheaval: How Nations Cope with Crisis and Change. Penguin Books Limited.

Eatwell, R. & Goodwin, M. (2018). National Populism: The Revolt Against Liberal Democracy. Penguin UK.

Media library (in German)

- GUDialog – Salafist propaganda on the web (an example for simplified answers for compex topics)
- The podcast on identity, pluralism and extremism of the RISE project (especially episode #03: Pluralism – "Pluralismus - Wie verstehen wir uns?") The Required Middle - Andreas Zick and Beate Küpper on Right-Wing Extremist and Right-Wing Populist Tendencies in Germany (The podcast on politics, society and history from Dietz-Verlag)
- Podcast "Wegweiser fragt nach": #1 Interview with Prof. Andreas Zick

Friedrich Gabel

Crisis management, normality and values

1. Introduction

When talking about improving crisis prevention and crisis management, we commonly think about further developing the development of technologies and structures. Dams are built higher and in more stable fashion, forecasting and early warning systems are refined and emergency forces are equipped more extensively for new situations. Although technical solutions contribute significantly to improving the way we deal with crises, in the course of improvement it should also be considered whether existing demands and ideas of "good" crisis management are still appropriate. "Appropriateness" as a value-related term refers to the fact that both the problems to be addressed and the measures provided to deal with them are shaped by social values and the result of democratic deliberation. At the centre of this negotiation lies the question: How much are we as a society prepared to invest in crisis management and crisis prevention? The values and assumptions about normality that these negotiations build upon influence what is determined as the goal of crisis management, what is considered a danger, who or what is determined as worthy of protection and who is seen as responsible for implementation processes. These presumptions set the framework for how individuals, organisations or societies act (in crises) and which possibilities for technical further development are perceived.

Along these questions, this article will examine the appropriateness of current crisis management and derive starting points for improvement, especially with regard to crisis prevention in Germany. The focus of this article is on the hypothesis that in the course of a further development crisis management, not only the technical questions but also the underlying values and concepts of normality should be critically scrutinized.

After all, not every technical development automatically represents an improvement. Rather, improvements should bring us closer to realizing our (societal) objectives.

The aim of this article is not to provide a general answer to these questions - the concrete contexts of action are too diverse - but rather to point out and discuss existing concepts of values and normality in current crisis management. At the same time, I argue, that explicit answers to these questions have to be discussed more continuously and explicitely in an ongoing democratic discourse.

The article is divided into six sections. After introducing the underlying understanding of values, concepts of normality as well as crises, four questions are examined more closely: (1) What is the goal of crisis management? (2) What is described as a danger and why? (3) Who or what is (particularly) worth protecting? (4) Who bears responsibility for crisis management? The article concludes by drawing together these considerations in view of the question: How much are we as a society prepared to invest in crisis management and crisis prevention?

2. The importance of values and concepts of normality for thinking about crises

Before looking more closely at value- and normality-related issues in dealing with crises, I will firstly explain what I mean when I speak of values, concepts of normality as well as crises and crisis management.

We constantly encounter values in everyday life. Particularly visible are material values, for example monetary values. On the selling side, the value formulates a target, a price to be achieved. It provides orientation, a value orientation, on how a sales talk should go. The situation is similar with ideational values. Ideational values provide orientation for individual, organisational or societal action; through values we define what we consider desirable. They, too, formulate a goal and allow us to draw conclusions about which action is right or, at least they point us roughly into a direction. Examples of ideational values include freedom, justice, security and efficiency. As these examples suggest, what is understood as a value not only differs depending on the person, organisation or society questioned. The meaning and status of individual values are also up for discussion. The sum of values of an individual, organisation or societal, as well as the norms, rules and attitudes attached to them are referred to as moral (conceptions) (Wiesing, 2012, p. 23).

Value or moral concepts neither have to be always explicit nor consciously known. Rather, they usually come under scrutiny when uncertainty about how to act in a specific situation prevails (Bayertz, 2004; Gabel, Mühleck, Krause, Schad & Rekowski, forthcoming). In this sense, crises and the challenges they bring can help to stimulate a discussion about values and moral concepts. Such moral uncertainty about the right course of action usually has one of two reasons: Either existing values and moral concepts do not provide sufficient orientation on how to act appropriately in a situation, or existing values and moral concepts come into conflict. The latter can be the case within a given value system or shared values come into conflict with each other. This might be the case, for instance, if one is faced with the question of whether to prioritise preserving freedoms or increasing security in a situation (Koch, 2014). Conflicting values may also arise in between individuals, organisations or societies. In both cases, the discussions on compulsory vaccination in the wake of the pandemic come to mind as an example (Deutscher Ethikrat, 2021).

Reflecting about moral concepts and moral problems is the subject of the discipline of ethics. On the one hand, ethics is concerned with assessing the legitimacy of arguments and associated courses of action in a methodically structured manner. On the other hand, ethics is dedicated to addressing questions such as What kind of world do we want to live in? or What kind of action is acceptable against the background of our values? (Ammicht Quinn, 2014).

To be differentiated but yet closely connected to values and moral concepts, are concepts of normality. Normality is a category designated to order social interaction. In its basic denotation it refers to what is expected or usual. It is defined by the demarcation from the non-normal or the extraordinary (Waldschmidt, 2005). What is considered "normal" also depends on the persons, organisations or societies surveyed and cannot be universally defined. The basis for determining what is "normal" in this sense is always a societal attibution within which experiences, measurements and calculations[1] are established. However, the determination of normality is a social construction, an interpretation of data in line with certain values. In this vein, normality (How is something?) is transformed into normativity (How should something be?) (Waldschmidt, 2005): What ought to be is derived from what is. The reference to "normality" is thus always an instrument of power and may have positive as well as negative consequences (Bigo, 2008).

Such Is-Ought problems are highly controversial within ethics (Pieper, 2007, p. 193). Some argue that empirical facts can inspire value concepts and provide arguments. However, whether something is valuable and desirable is not an empirical but an ethical question. To illustrate what this has to do with the topic of this collection, a brief example might be given: the fact that 10-, 100-, 1000- and 10,000-year floods exist, offers no indication as to which of these events individuals, organisations or societies should prepare for. The latter is, in the best case, based on a democratic debate representing all affected persons.

This brings me back to the understanding of crises and crisis management. In the context of this paper, crises are understood as situations of acute threat to values and living conditions of individuals, organisations or societies in which action to avert a disaster is still possible (see e.g. Boin & Hart, 2007, p. 42). Crisis and disaster management thus describe similar and largely overlapping areas, which, however, assume a different state of emergency.

Hence, with regard to normality, an ambivalent picture emerges. On the one hand, crises represent a break with normality; on the other hand, it is debatable to what extent the occurrence of crises is in itself part of normality (Gross & Weichselgartner, 2015, p. 14). While crises per se cannot be avoided, it can be assumed that specific events such as floods or droughts can be better avoided through technology and strategy, shifting the crisis threshold.

This minimal definition contains two aspects that are of fundamental importance for further consideration: First, that the existence of crises depends on what is determined as normality and what measures are taken

1 "Calculated" suggest a certain degree of objectivity which should be critically scrutinized in three ways: regarding the criterion used for classifying something as normal and its justification, the defined level of distribution in order to be considered normal, and the extent to which survey methods themselves are shaped by presuppositions about what is to be measured or calculated.

in this context; crises are relative. Whether a certain water level is normal depends on the context and the observing entity. What is considered normal for the Nile River, would be understood as an extreme event of possibly catastrophic proportions in Germany due to previous experience and geographical circumstances. Second, crises have a societal history. Depending on what an individual, an organisation or a society sets as normality, and depending on the measures that are taken along with it, an event that takes place may or may not constitute a crisis, and a crisis may or may not become a catastrophe, respectively.

Based on these understandings, various value- and normality-related nuances of the question "What and how much are we as a society prepared to invest in prevention, preparedness and management?" are considered in the following section.

3. What is determined as the goal of crisis management?

The quality of any improvement in crisis management must be measured by the extent to which it meets the overarching goal of crisis management. But what is the goal of crisis management? This question may seem baffling at first glance, since it appears to be established that it is concerned with the successful prevention of, provision for, management of and recovery from crises. However, if considerig more closely the developments and findings of disaster research over the past 50 years, it becomes clear that there is more than one interpretation of the above description and, consequently, what might be considered good prevention of, provision for, management of and recovery from crisis.

Sociologist Kathleen Tierney, for example, argues for an increased understanding of disasters – although this seems to be applicable to crises, as well – as co-constructed and co-produced in recent decades (Tierney, 2019, p. 66). By co-construction, Tierney refers to the observation that what counts as a disaster is not simply given, but is socially (especially politically) determined (Pohlmann, 2015). Depending on the observer, one and the same event can be described as an extreme event, a crisis or a disaster. For instance, the Covid-19 pandemic was only declared a disaster in one out of the sixteen German states, Bavaria (Bayerische Staatsregierung, 2020). In this sense, it is not simply the quantifiable level, the extent, the damage or the number of victims that makes an event a crisis or disaster. What counts as a crisis or a disaster is in fact a societal, a political decision by which necessities for certain actions and priorities are determined. This decision depends on previous experiences, associated notions of normality as well as societal values. In addition, speaking of crises and disasters depicts a special existential threat which to overcome demands extraordinary measures and a special political scope for action and thus entails legitimising potential for political action (Wæver, 1995).

The hypothesis of a societal co-production of crises and disasters also points to a societal co-responsibility for the emergence of crises and disasters, which becomes manifest in at least two ways. On the one hand, co-responsibility stems from contributory negligence. Examples include accidents involving high-risk technologies (such as nuclear power plants) or the increase in extreme events as a result of human-made climate change (Guyer, 2019). On the other hand, societal co-responsibility refers to insufficient societal action.

Here, the concept of vulnerability is of crucial importance. Simply speaking, vulnerability describes the susceptibility of an entity to a danger (Wisner, Blaikie, Cannon & Davis, 2004). With regard to crisis management, the concept of vulnerability represents the conviction that crises and disasters do not necessarily follow from specific (natural) events, but are the result of an interaction between manifesting hazards and more or less vulnerable societal structures (Birkmann, 2008, p. 6; Gabel, 2019; Wisner, Blaikie, Cannon & Davis, 2004, p. 10).

Three key implications follow from this argument: First, that crises and disasters do not "simply" result from events, but that it depends on the person, organisation or society facing an event. Depending on their (lack of) capacities, which arise from the interplay of existing characteristics as well as the type and degree of prevention and preparedness measures, crises and disasters can (not) be avoided effectively. Against the backdrop of this argument, the United Nations Sendai Framework has shifted the international objective towards reducing the risk of disasters (UN-ISDR, 2015).

Second, the argument of being able to influence vulnerability raises the question of needing to influence or even having to influence, which refers to the question when and where crisis management should take place. For decades, disaster research in particular has argued that crises and disasters reinforce disadvantages and vulnerabilities that already exist in everyday life. Thus, disaster research emphasises the need to think of crises and disasters from the perspective of everyday actions (Dombrowsky & Brauner, 1996). People, organisations or even societies that are already struggling with existential problems in everyday life will very likely be less well equipped to prevent crises and disasters. They will be less able to take precautions and thus struggle to respond. However, social policy and crisis management are still very much separate spheres, both with regard to concrete tasks and the responsibility of various actors (Gabel, 2019).

A third implication regarding the goal of crisis management arises in respect to the concept of resilience. Due to the absence of a universal definition, resilience here is understood as the ability of an entity (e.g. people, animals, organisations, societies) to survive crises and disasters. Unlike protective measures against extreme events, which is the focus of security action, resilience aims at building capacities to deal with manifesting extreme events (Krüger, 2019a). Resilience embodies the view that not every threat event can be avoided. Resilience therefore should be understood as complementary to "classical" security action (Krüger, 2019b, p. 59), which additionally has to be improved as part of crisis management.[2]

Finally, in approaching all these questions, one should also critically reflect on societal narratives of crisis and disaster (Horn, 2010). For example, the argument that not everyone can be saved in crises and disasters can be mentioned here. Although such statements may be true in retrospect, it is problematic to (un)consciously turn them into a goal and to rashly "accept" casualties .

4. What is described as a danger and why?

Closely related to the question on the goal of crisis management is the question of which dangers are to be considered, prevented or overcome for the purpose of crisis management. This question contains at least two dimensions: What is described as a danger? What does a danger mean for whom?

2 Against this backdrop, resilience cannot simply be understood as the opposite of vulnerabililty. Considering vulnerability as multidimensional, an entity can be vulnerable in one regard butresilient in another. Such an understanding is helpful to counteract a tendency to render abilities invisible in light of existing vulnerabilities.

With regard to the first question, considering the co-construction of crises and disasters, it might be agued that extreme events, crises and disasters are patterns of interpretation which may differ between societies and within societies. Whether and in what way an event or an entity is considered a danger is a political question which mostly refers but not necessarily corresponds with a real threat scenario. For example, the topic of migration is worth mentioning here. On the one hand, recently there has been a renewed increase in arguments describing migration as a danger that is not only to be prevented using security measures, but also through civil protection measures (Baumann, Lorenz & Rosenow, 2011). On the other hand, the insecurity of refugees and their vulnerability are increasingly at risk of taking a back seat (McDonald, 2016). Moreover, any talk about preventing or overcoming dangers reflects a more-or-less appropriate prioritisation, depending on the situation. Examples for this are not only the insufficient counter-measures taken in response to the threat of a pandemic caused by a Corona virus which had been extensively described since 2012 (Deutscher Bundestag, 2012; Mukerji & Mannino, 2020). In light of the ongoing climate crisis, hazards such as forest fires and draughts are increasingly manifesting in Germany, as well (Guyer, 2019). These new threats call for a swift development of prevention, preparedness and coping strategies, and to equip them with adequate resources.

In context of the second question of what a certain danger means for whom, it can then be critically examined that the threat character of events is perspective-dependent. Here, the previously mentioned example of the Nile comes to mind again. Its periodic floods are primarily an empirical fact. Societally speaking, however, it is not only understood as a danger to life and limb, but also as a necessity for life in this region. The interpretation of this fact is thus dependent on the respective perspective. Such an awareness of the dependence of hazard interpretations on different perspectives is of societal relevance. On the one hand, because dangers sometimes manifest very differently for different groups of people and may entail a very unequal threat potential. On the other hand, because (perceived) dangers can differ between different group of people. Here, too, reference can be made to the topic of migration. Hence, it is globally acknowledged that people without residence permits are particularly at risk in crises and disasters, as they are rarely reached by aid measures (Anonymus, 2006; Orru, Hansson, Gabel, Tammpuu, Krüger, Savadori, Meyer, Torpan, Jukarainen, Schieffelers, Lovasz & Rhinard,

2022). Among the reasons for this is also a distrust toward state organs, the fear of being expelled or even experiencing racially motivated violence (Tierney, 2019, p. 162). Previous counter-measures have mostly been limited to identifying this lack of trust as a problem, instead of acknowledging that this existing danger of losing perceived opportunities for a good life is an understandable assessment. This also entails questions, such as who can afford what level of trust in the system and who faces the danger of being forgotten.

5. Who or what is (particularly) worth protecting?

Thirdly, with regard to the aim of a further development of crisis management, concepts of value and normality can be considered with regard to the question of what should be regarded worthy of protection in a crisis or disaster. This question, which has once again gained attention in the context of the pandemic, unfolds its importance not only in its answer, but already in its formulation: Is being discussed who or what is worth protecting, or who or what is particularly worth protecting?

Initially, I'd like to attend to the question of whether there is or should be something or someone in crises that is not worth protecting. By way of example, four aspects of approaching this question are illustrated below. The first unfolds along the general question to what extent crises and disasters display issues that are at least partly to blame for their occurrence (Fainstein, 2015). In view of the year 2022, the energy crisis could be mentioned as an example. In its context, the search for alternative gas suppliers was weighed against the increased expansion of renewable energies (Hummel, 2022).

A second aspect arises with regard to the worthiness of protection of cultural values. In addition to the protection of cultural objects this also concerns the worthiness of protecting societal values. This aspect is reflected, for instance in the debates on the value of data protection in the efforts to combat the Coronavirus pandemic (Bernau, 2020; linus, 2020). It was argued that strong data protection would make it difficult to trace chains of infection and is therefore not appropriate in the course of pandemic management. Although it does not seem very plausible to simply throw out well-founded, proven and widely accepted everyday values in crises, this case shows that it may well be necessary to critically examine the appropriateness of values (but also conceptions of normality) as well as their evaluation in crisis situations (Gabel, Mühleck, Krause, Schad & Rekowski, forthcoming; Krause & Wezel, 2022; Mukerji & Mannino, 2020).

In line with a third aspect, the question of worthiness of protection can, in principle, also be posed with regard to groups of persons: Are there people who are not worthy of protection? Against the background of a constitutional state based on the concept of human dignity and in view of the claim of humanitarian principles to reduce suffering regardless of individual characteristics, this question must in principle be negated. However, this question points to areas of tension that crisis management must address. For instance, regarding the topic of medical triage. In the absence of sufficient capacities, a justification must be given for prioritised care for people who are generally speaking equally worthy of protection (Mannino, 2021). Other examples include situations in which emergency forces are confronted with the complicity of people in crises (terrorists, combatants, etc.). Thus, the implementation of the central humanitarian principle to provide assistance in a neutral, independent and impartial way based solely on the suffering of those affected goes hand in hand with comprehensive demands regarding the professional behaviour of emergency forces (Gabel, Mühleck, Krause, Schad & Rekowski, forthcoming). How difficult these are to meet at times, is shown not at last in the operations of aid organisations in the context of the war in Ukraine (Kahlweit & Pfaff, 2022).

A final aspect relating to concepts of value and normality to be discussed here is the (non-)worthiness of protection of other entities. Due to an increasing expansion of our moral frame to include animals, plants and the environment, crisis management is also faced with the question of whether and to what extent the conditions of existence for animals, plants or the broader environment - for their own sake, and not "merely" as an economic factor - should be considered more strongly (Gabel, Mühleck, Krause, Schad & Rekowski, forthcoming).

In addition to the discussion about a fundamental worthiness of protection, the question of prioritisation also arises within the group(s) considered: Who is particularly worthy of protection in crises? Based on the underlying understanding of "worthiness" and the reference object (worthy of protection, why and in what sense?), two different aspects can be distinguished here: Worthiness of protection due to a special need for protection or worthiness of protection in the sense of importance for the maintenance of the social system.

The need for protection refers to the respective vulnerability (see above) of an entity. In line with modern approaches to vulnerability, this is not derived deterministically from certain individual characteristics, such as age, gender, existing impairments or the socio-economic situation, but instead results from the complex and intersectional interplay of these characteristics and the respective social structure (Kuran, Morsut, Kruke, Krüger, Segnestam, Orru, Nævestad, Airola, Keränen, Gabel, Hansson & Torpan, 2020; Wisner, Blaikie, Cannon & Davis, 2004). Thus, social structures influence whether and to what extent impairments become disabilities and are associated with restrictions in societal participation. At the same time, vulnerability arises situationally, i.e. out of the acute interaction of characteristics with a specific situation or hazardous situation. In this sense, vulnerability should not be understood as static and unchangeable like the talk of "vulnerable groups" suggests (Gabel, 2019; Kailes, 2015). The relevance of these considerations for the appropriateness of crisis management is reflected, for example, in a report by the United Nations (UN, 2020, p. 15). According to this, the elderly, people with disabilities, children, women, migrants and refugees were particularly vulnerable in the Coronavirus pandemic. Taking into consideration the previously presented argument that vulnerability arises to a large extent from social action and social structures, the question arises, whether these are in an unreasonable manner designed for non-migrant white men without disabilities or chronic illnesses between the ages of 18 and 65. In light of this, efforts to improve crisis management should also critically question its underlying conception of the human being (Gabel, Krüger, Morsut & Kuran, 2022).

Important for the maintenance of a system (systemrelevant), on the other hand, are actors that fulfill essential functions in, for example, a society (Villa, 2020). Both persons or (critical) infrastructures can be described as important for the maintenance of a system. The latter comprises areas, the former refers to the people working in these structures. Currently, in Germany, the areas include: Energy, food, finance and insurance, health, information technology and telecommunications, media and culture, municipal waste disposal, government and administration, transport and traffic, and water (BBK & BSI, 2021). The question of appropriateness and existing values arises here, for example, in the "education" sector, which has not yet been mentioned. Negative consequences for pupils, trainees and students as a result of the pandemic-related closure of educational institutions, both formal (schools and universities) and informal (e.g. youth work), are becoming increasingly visible and problematic (Deutscher Ethikrat, 2022; Karutz, 2022).

6. Who bears responsibility for crisis management?

Finally, in the context of striving for a further development of crisis management, the very concepts of values and normality should be critically examined. In general, it can be stated that in the described discussion of concepts such as vulnerability or resilience, increasing responsibility has been attributed to societal action in recent decades (Krüger & Gabel, 2022): On the one hand, in the sense of the co-production of crises and disasters through the design of social structures. On the other hand, by means of their associated power to avoid and prevent crises and disasters. Both suggest that modern crisis management can and should act much more proactively with regard to improving everyday life structures and reducing social disparities. This can be specified by looking at two questions: Which actors should be considered in the context of crisis management? In what fashion this should be done.

With regard to the actors, for example, in Germany, a country whose crisis management is to a large degree is based on voluntary commitment, the question arises as to whether these structures are still sufficient for sustainable crisis management in larger, long-lasting and interconnected situations. This is especially true in light of a changing, diversifying and in the coming years very likely also shrinking volunteer commitment (Markert, 2021). Against this backdrop, the self-help capacities of the population are increasingly becoming a focus of attention.

When it comes to the question how actors are included, the critical consideration of anthropological ideas and stereotypes is of central concern. This can also be exemplified with regard to the general population. Indeed, in current crisis management, the population is usually portrayed as a homogeneous, passive, ill-prepared and sometimes even disruptive actor with regard to situation management (Geenen, 2010; Schulze, Lorenz & Wenzel, 2015). This is critical in several respects: First, the perception of population groups as passive on the one hand and disruptive on the other is ambivalent. It reflects a central area of tension in current crisis management. There is an increasing demand for a more active population and its self-governance in response to crises (Sticher & Ohder, 2013). In contrast to this, independent civic participation is still seen to a large extent as disruptive - for example through the establishment of parallel structures for spontaneous assistance – within a clearly hierarchised and highly structured civil protection body (Krüger & Albris, 2021). One reason for this is not least the lack of structures for cooperation.

Secondly, the wording of "the population" (die Bevölkerung) is to be scruitinized in the course of improving crisis response. Against the backdrop of an increasing awareness for the diversity of different population groups and the persons they comprise, it seems almost contradictory to speak of the population as an apparently "homogeneous entity". This can be seen concretely, for example, in the different capacities people maintain due to their diverse life situations which, again, are co-produced by societal action. Furthermore, the phrasing "the population" is irritating because it suggests a separation of crisis management and population. Yet the people involved in crisis management are also part of the population. In this sense, they find themselves in various life situations, are exposed to conflicting responsibilities (Who takes care of children and relatives requiring care so that emergency forces can do their duties?) or experience value conflicts between their convictions and mission mandates.

Third, speaking of an ill-prepared and passive population obscures both differences and the reasons underlying different capacities. For example, the aforementioned demands for preparedness or an increase in resilience are accompanied by very different challenges depending on the life situation. What is normal varies vastly for different persons because of their own socialisation, occupation and previous experience. This is not only reflected financially or spatially, but also in terms of prior knowledge or the availability of resources such as attention and time. For example, the question arises to what extent the BBK checklist for disaster preparedness is fit to address diverse life situations and/or whether it should provide structures to support individual preparedness (BBK, 2019; Gabel, 2019). This also refers to the ethical principle that, with regard to the attribution of responsibility for action, a *ought-to-do* always presupposes a *can-do*. If entities are not capable of doing something, it is not ethically legitimate to ascribe responsibility for that task to them (Rosoff, 2015, p. 6). Conversely, it should be analysed, whether current attributions of responsibility are underpinned by the corresponding capacities of the responsible actors or, if not, whether steps have been taken to empower these actors.

If all three attributions are taken together, it can be discussed to what extent these descriptions are still appropriate or if they ever were.

7. Aspects of a critical (re)consideration of concepts of values and normality in crises management

In the previous pages, it was argued that a further development of crisis management is not only a question of better technologies, but also requires a critical examination of the "appropriateness" of underlying values and concepts of normality. Within four guiding questions, various examples were presented to show where concepts of value and normality play a role in how our society deals with crises and disasters and what issues further development faces, both theoretically and practically. A central point is made by the argument that crises and disasters are both socially co-constructed and to a large extent co-produced by societal (non-) action. Based on these considerations, I now present some guiding questions that should be considered in the future development of crisis management, especially with regard to the prevention of crises and disasters.

What is determined as the goal of crisis management?

- On what basis were previous events (not) described as a crisis or disaster and by whom?
- Is crisis management aimed at preventing events (e.g. floods, blackouts, health emergencies, supply shortages) or at building capacities to respond?
- What are legitimate limits to prevention and preparedness and what skills are required for the (e.g. individual) survival of a crisis or disaster?
- To what extent is the dismantling of disadvantaging or discriminating social structures considered in crisis and disaster management?
- Does crisis management follow the goal of trying to save each individual or is being discussed who cannot be saved?

What is described as a danger that needs to be considered, prevented or managed and why?

- With regard to planning: What has (not) been described as a potential crisis or disaster and therefore has become available for political discussion and action?
- To what extent is the appropriateness of framing social issues as security problems critically interrogated (for instance in the case of migration)?
- To what extent are differences in experiencing dangerous situations taken into account?
- To what extent are the reasons for distrust understood as illegitimate interference or deficits in government action?

Who or what is described as (particularly) worthy of protection?

- To what extent is it considered that existing social structures might no longer be appropriate, timely and worthy of protection?
- To what extent do values common in everyday life need to be protected and/or adapted in crises and disasters and how are deviations justified?
- How is equal worthiness of protection of all individuals in situations of scarcity accounted for?
- To what extent do other entities, such as animals or plants, have to be taken into account in crisis management?
- Is the idea of human nature underlying current crisis management appropriate to the existing diversity of society?
- Which sectors are (not) designated as critical infrastructure or systemically relevant and why

Who bears responsibility for crisis management?

- To what extent are current ways of attributing responsibility for crisis management known and appropriate? Are entities able to do what they are supposed to do?
- To what extent are different life situations, levels of affectednes and capacities - for precautions or building resilience - taken into account in the ways responsibility is attributed?
- What ideas exist about certain actors in crisis management - for example, the population - and to what extent are these appropriate?
- To what extent is independent action by actors recognised and why (not)?

All these questions and the aspects associated with them, such as an increase in critical reflection, improved consideration of societal diversity or a larger number of entities to be taken into account, ultimately point towards a need for an increase in resources for the value-related improvement of crisis management.

In light of extreme events, crises and military conflicts that affect Germany in particular, this once again raises the question "*How much should we as a society be willing to invest in crisis management and crisis prevention?*". So far, this question has either been raised and discussed implicitly or purely in relation to individual measures without formulating broader strategic goals.

However, the past few years may offer an opportunity to engage with it more strongly than before as a socio-political question and to discuss it explicitly and with the participation of the population. The "German Strategy for Strengthening Resilience to Disasters" published in July 2022 can only be a first step in this direction (BMI, 2022), which must be filled with life, especially with regard to the demand for more participation.

8. Bibliography

Ammicht Quinn, R. (2014). Security ethics: An introduction. In R. Ammicht Quinn (Ed.), Studies in homeland security: vol. 16. security ethics (pp. 15-47). Springer VS.

Anonymous (2006). Vulnerable Populations: Who are They. American Journal of Managed Care, 12(13), 348-352. http://www.ajmc.com/publications/supplement/2006/2006-11-vol12-n13suppl/nov06- 2390ps348-s352

Baumann, M., Lorenz, A. & Rosenow, K. (2011). Linking Immigration Policies and Migrants' Journeys: An Interdisciplinary Endeavor. In M. Baumann, A. Lorenz & K. Rosenow (Eds.), Crossing and Controlling Borders (pp. 9-20).

Bavarian State Government (ed.). (2020, 16 March). Press releases: Corona pandemic / Bavaria declares state of emergency / Event bans and operating prohibitions. https://www.bayern.de/corona-pandemie-bayern-ruft-den-katastrophenfall-aus-veranstaltungsverbote-und-betriebsuntersagungen/

Bayertz, K. (2004). On the self-enlightenment of applied ethics. In H. Friesen & K. Berr (Eds.), Practical philosophy controversial: Vol. 2. Applied ethics in the field of tension between justification and application (pp. 51-73). Lang.

BBK. (2019). Guidebook for emergency preparedness and proper action in emergency situations.

BBK & BSI. (06.2021). Critical Infrastructures - Sector and Industry Classification: Status July 2021. https://www.bbk.bund.de/SharedDocs/Downloads/DE/KRITIS/kritis-sektoren-brancheneinteilung.pdf?__blob=publicationFile&v=3

Bernau, P. (1 August 2020). The state obstructs the Corona app: commentary. FAZ. https://www.faz.net/aktuell/wirtschaft/die-corona-app-hat-zu-viel-datenschutz-doch-der-ist-noetig-16886030.html

Bigo, D. (2008). Security: A Field Left Fallow. In M. Dillon & A. W. Neal (Eds.), Foucault on Politics, Security and War (pp. 93-114). Palgrave Macmillan.

Birkmann, J. (2008). Global environmental change, natural hazards, vulnerability and disaster resilience. Spatial Research and Planning, 66(1), 5-22. https://doi.org/10.1007/BF03184043

BMI. (2022). German strategy for strengthening resilience to disasters. Berlin.

Boin, A. & Hart, P. '. (2007). The Crisis Approach. In H. Rodríguez, E. L. Quarantelli & R. R. Dynes (Eds.), Handbooks of sociology and social research. Handbook of disaster research (pp. 42-54). Springer.

German Bundestag (ed.). (2012). Report on risk analysis in civil protection 2012: German Bundestag, 17th legislative period. Printed Paper 17/12051.

German Ethics Council (ed.). (2021). Ethical orientation on the question of a general statutory vaccination requirement: ad hoc recommendation. Berlin.

German Ethics Council (ed.). (2022, 28 November). Pandemic and mental health: attention, assistance and support for children, adolescents and young adults in and after social crises. Ad Hoc Recommendation. Berlin.

Dombrowsky, W. R. & Brauner, C. (1996). Deficits of disaster preparedness in industrial societies using the example of Germany. Studies and recommendations on basic methodological and content-related questions: Expert report commissioned by the German IDNDR Committee for Disaster Prevention e.V. (long version) (German

IDNDR Series 3b). https://www.bbk.bund.de/SharedDocs/Downloads/BBK/DE/FIS/DownloadsInformationsangebote/Downloads-KritischeInfrastrukturen/DownloadsProjekte/Katastrophenschutz-GutachtenNotfallseelsorge.pdf?__blob=publicationFile

Fainstein, S. (2015). Resilience and Justice. International Journal of Urban and Regional Research, 39(1), 157-167. https://doi.org/10.1111/1468-2427.12186

Gabel, F. (2019). Opportunities of dynamic conceptions of vulnerability for disaster management. In M. Krüger & M. Max (Eds.), Society of difference: vol. 46. resilience in disaster: concepts for strengthening those in need of care and assistance in civil protection (1st ed., pp. 77-96). transcript.

Gabel, F., Krüger, M., Morsut, C. & Kuran, C. H. A. (2022). Bridging the Gap between Vulnerable Groups and Vulnerable Situations: Towards an Integrative Perspective New Assessment on Vulnerability for Disaster Risk Reduction: Contributing Paper for Global Assessment Report on Disaster Risk Reduction 2022. Geneva. https://www.undrr.org/publication/bridging-gap-between-vulnerable-groups-and-vulnerable-situations-towards-integrative

Gabel, F., Mühleck, M., Krause, K., Schad, J. & Rekowski, M. (forthcoming). Ethische Reflexion im Bevölkerungsschutz: Leitfaden für eine ethisch reflektierte Entscheidungsfindung im Sanitäts- und Betreuungsdienst, ed. by BBK.

Geenen, E. M. (2010). Population behaviour and possibilities of crisis management and disaster management in multicultural societies. Research in Civil Protection: Vol. 11. Federal Office for Civil Protection and Disaster Assistance.

Gross, B. & Weichselgartner, J. (2015). Modern risk management: Between robustness and resilience. BBK: Population Protection - Natural Hazards(1), 12-17.

Guyer, M. (2019). Consequences of global climate change for Germany: First partial report: An overview of the impact chains. 20/2019.

Horn, E. (2010). Ends of people: Global catastrophes as biopolitical fantasy. In R. Sorg & S. B. Würffel (Eds.), Utopia and apocalypse in modernity (pp. 101-118). Fink.

Hummel, T. (23 March 2022). The debates Germany is having on energy issues are absurd. Süddeutsche.de. https://www.sueddeutsche.de/meinung/energiewende-deutschland-kommentar-1.5553078

Kahlweit, C. & Pfaff, I. (31 December 2022). The dilemma of the Red Cross. Süddeutsche.de. https://www.sueddeutsche.de/politik/ukraine-rotes-kreuz-russland-1.5557232?reduced=true

Kailes, J. I. (2015). If people would just prepare! In I. Kelman & L. M.

Stough (Eds.), Disability and disaster: Explorations and exchanges (pp. 97-109). Palgrave Macmillan.

Karutz, H. (16 February 2022). Counting educational institutions as critical infrastructure. FAZ. https://www.faz.net/aktuell/karriere-hochschule/warum-schulen-als-kritische-infrastruktur-gelten-sollten-17811150.html

Koch, H. (2014). Freedom and security. In R. Ammicht Quinn (Ed.), Studies in homeland security: vol. 16. security ethics (pp. 135-144). Springer VS.

Krause, K. & Wezel, K. (2022). Security from what and for whom? Security in the pandemic. In Studies in Internal Security. Politics between power and powerlessness: On the political handling of the Corona pandemic in Germany (pp. 363-394). Springer VS.

Krüger, M. (2019a). Building Instead of Imposing Resilience: Revisiting the Relationship Between Resilience and the State. International Political Sociology, 13(1), 53-67. https://doi.org/10.1093/ips/oly025

Krüger, M. (2019b). Resilience: Between state demand and societal promotion. In M. Krüger & M. Max (Eds.), Society of difference: vol. 46. Resilience in disasters: concepts for empowering those in need of care and assistance in civil protection (1st ed., pp. 57-76). transcript.

Krüger, M. & Albris, K. (2021). Resilience unwanted: Between control and cooperation in disaster response. Security Dialogue, 52(4), 343-360. https://doi.org/10.1177/0967010620952606

Krüger, M. & Gabel, F. (2022). From Lisbon to Sendai: Responsibilities in International Disaster Management. In H. Hansen-Magnusson & A. Vetterlein (Eds.), Routledge handbooks. The Routledge handbook on responsibility in international relations (pp. 203-216). Routledge Taylor & Francis Group.

Kuran, C. H. A., Morsut, C., Kruke, B. I., Krüger, M., Segnestam, L., Orru, K., Nævestad, T. O., Airola, M., Keränen, J., Gabel, F., Hansson, S. & Torpan, S. (2020). Vulnerability and vulnerable groups from an intersectionality perspective. International Journal of Disaster Risk Reduction, 50, 101826. https://doi.org/10.1016/j.ijdrr.2020.101826

linus. (2020, 6 April). 10 touchstones for assessing "contact tracing" apps. https://www.ccc.de/de/updates/2020/contact-tracing-requirements

Mannino, A. (2021). Who do I save - and if so, how many? On triage and distributive justice. (What does it all mean?): No. 14068. Reclam.

Markert, R. T. (2021, 4 July). Advertising volunteerism: disaster relief in need? https://www.zdf.de/nachrichten/panorama/katastrophen-schutz-ehrenamt-werbung-100.html

McDonald, M. (2016). Whose security? Ethics and the referent. In J. Nyman & A. Burke (Eds.), Routledge critical security studies series. Ethical security studies: A new research agenda (1st ed., pp. 32-45). Routledge Taylor & Francis Group.

Mukerji, N. & Mannino, A. (2020). Covid-19: What matters in crisis: On philosophy in real time. Reclam's Universal Library.

Orru, K., Hansson, S., Gabel, F., Tammpuu, P., Krüger, M., Savadori, L., Meyer, S. F., Torpan, S., Jukarainen, P., Schieffelers, A., Lovasz, G. & Rhinard, M. (2022). Approaches to 'vulnerability' in eight European disaster management systems. Disasters, 46(3), 742-767. https://doi.org/10.1111/disa.12481

Pieper, A. (2007). Introduction to ethics. UTB für Wissenschaft Uni-Taschenbücher Philosophie: Vol. 1637. A. Francke Verlag.

Pohlmann, K. (2015). Priority setting in disaster management. In H.-J. Lange & C. Gusy (Eds.), Cooperation in disaster and civil protection (pp. 213-287). Springer Fachmedien Wiesbaden.

Rosoff, P. M. (2015). In defence of (some) altered standards of care for Ebola infections in developed countries. HEC forum : an interdisciplinary journal on hospitals' ethical and legal issues, 27(1), 1-9.

Schulze, K., Lorenz, D. F. & Wenzel, B. (2015). Population behaviour in disasters: Potentially helpful. Emergency Preparedness, 2015(01), 21-28. expert editorial, WALHALLA.

Sticher, B. & Ohder, C. (2013). Involving the population in disaster management. SIAK-Jounal - Journal of Police Science and Practice(2/2013), 81-93.

Tierney, K. J. (2019). Disasters: a sociological approach. Polity Press.

UN. (2020). The Sustainable Development Goals Report 2020. United Nations publication.

UN-ISDR. (2015). Sendai Framework for Disaster Risk Reduction 2015-2030. http://www.unisdr.org/files/43291_sendaiframeworkfor-drren.pdf

Villa, P.-I. (2020). Corona crisis meets care crisis - Is it systemic? Leviathan, 48(3), 433-450. https://doi.org/10.5771/0340-0425-2020-3-433

Wæver, O. (1995). Securitization and desecuritization. In R. D. Lipschutz (Ed.), New directions in world politics. On security (pp. 46-86). Columbia University Press.

Waldschmidt, A. (2005). Disability policy in the tension between standardisation and normalisation. In S. Graumann & K. Grüber (Eds.),

Friedrichshain Colloquium: Vol. 2. Recognition, Ethics and Disability: Contributions from the Institute Man, Ethics and Science (pp. 175-194). Lit-Verl.

Wiesing, U. (ed.). (2012). Reclams universal library: No. 18963. ethics in medicine: a study book (4th ed.). Reclam.

Wisner, B., Blaikie, P., Cannon, T. & Davis, I. (2004). At risk: Natural hazards, people's vulnerability and disasters (2nd ed.). Routledge.

For further reading

- Ammicht Quinn, R. (ed.). (2014). Studies in homeland security: vol. 16. security ethics. Springer VS.
- Horn, E. (2014). Future as catastrophe. Frankfurt am Main: Fischer.
- Zack, N. (2011). Ethics for disaster. First paperback edition. Lanham: Rowman & Littlefield Publishers, Inc (Studies in social, political, and legal philosophy).

Media library

- SWR Knowledge. Crisis Preparedness: Can Disasters Be Planned?, URL: https://www.youtube.com/watch?v=kTTYRncU5LY
- NDR. Der Tatortreiniger, Staffel 4, Folge 3, Damit muss man rechnen

Alexander Fekete, Chris Hetkämper, Carlotta Bauer

Resilience in the Context of Civil Protection and Municipalities

1. Background and conceptual classification

Crisis resilience at the municipal level encompasses several disciplines that differ not only in terms of their concrete crisis objects, but also in their perspectives on crisis resilience. At the municipal level, several disciplines and thus also perspectives on resilience converge. On the one hand, there is an urban planning perspective, which is also examined in research in the context of so-called urban resilience. This involves settlement areas and typical perspectives from a spatial planning, urban planning or architectural perspective (Coaffee & Lee, 2017). Resilience is the longer-term design of the coexistence and functioning of cities as well as rural communities. This view, as well as a view in the environmental sciences, is influenced by the definition of resilience in ecology or ecosystem research (Gunderson & Holling, 2002; Holling, 1973). In this, resilience is understood as a study of the stability and dynamic development of environmental systems. Resilience is a fluctuating behaviour that, in contrast to a linear understanding of evolution, involves leaps, changes and collapses, while maintaining the core of the system, i.e. the functionality of the community in this case. The motto of the city of Paris with its municipal coat of arms expresses this understanding quite well: "It may fluctuate, but it will not perish" (fluctuat nec mergitur).

Another perspective on the definition of resilience in a municipal context is that of community resilience (S. L. Cutter et al., 2008; Norris, Stevens, Pfefferbaum, Wyche, & Pfefferbaum, 2008; Tobin, 1999). It is the set of factors or capabilities of a community or group of people, or indeed of an administrative unit such as a municipality, to deal with crisis and change. This includes the totality of all capabilities before, during and after a crisis, and a variety of types from rather passive absorption and resilience to progressive adaptation or even transformational capacity (UNDRR, 2022). There are certainly similarities in this understanding to the psychological understanding of resilience (see also the contributions by Dreßing and Gilan & Helmreich in this volume) and thus also to crisis management capacity, which can also be found in medicine, for example.

Another definition of the term in the municipal context is a scientific or engineering perspective, which understands resilience as a computational variable primarily with regard to the resilience and recovery capacity of material structures such as infrastructure or the built environment (Bogardi & Fekete, 2018). While vulnerability describes the degree of susceptibility to damage, resilience represents the degree or speed of recovery.

In the course of urban resilience or community resilience, however, the ability to transform is also increasingly emphasised, and it is possible that municipal resilience is also characterised by the ability to respond flexibly to constant change (Pelling, 2003, 2010). This approach draws on considerations from complexity research and understands the interaction between people and the environment as a complex, adaptive system (Becker, 2014), whose components pursue very different goals while constantly interacting with each other (Heylighen, Cilliers, & Gershenson, 2006). This approach suggests that there is no equilibrium in the sense of an optimally balanced state, rather the system is characterised by constant change (Pendall, Foster, & Cowell, 2010). The ability to continuously adapt to new conditions is resilience (Bergström & Dekker, 2014).

Cases of application of municipal resilience can be found on the one hand in response to various crises and hazards: to relatively sudden floods and other natural hazards as well as those of a different kind, such as the banking crisis, or also in the longer term in response to insidious risks or crises such as those related to climate change or in response to a pandemic. However, resilience is also an important issue in dealing with transformations such as the switch of municipalities to renewable energy or in response to ageing and the transformation of society through digitalisation (Fekete, 2022; Fekete & Rhyner, 2020).

2. Cities and municipalities in the context of crises and resilience

The Hyogo Framework from 2005 already presents the development and strengthening of capacities at the municipal level as a prerequisite for crisis resilience and calls for corresponding activities (UN/ISDR, 2005). Capacities can be understood as the totality of existing strategies, systems, resources and capabilities. These can be addressed at the institutional, organisational or individual level, but always interact with each other (CaDRI, 2011; Schulz, Gustafsson, & Illes, 2005). In order to successfully develop capacities, it is necessary to first understand the local context and the capacities that already exist (Hagelsteen & Burke, 2016). Relevant questions here are, for example, whether the local development strategy and legal framework support strengthening crisis resilience, whether organisations and businesses have financial and material resources and crisis-proof management systems, and whether employees or residents have relevant experience and skills to participate in community resilience-building processes.

Resilience is often discussed in terms of change processes in the management or governance of municipalities. For example, if a paradigm shift is to be made in disaster management or civil protection, away from a purely hazard-based approach and the protection of critical infrastructure towards resilience, then certain aspects of renewal are often listed here: Cross-sectoral or cross-silo thinking and thus much broader interdisciplinary collaboration between disciplines. This reflects a move away from pure specialism towards more generalism, as it can also be understood as a move away from 100% security promises or protection towards an accepted way of dealing with uncertainties. Individual expertise and specialists are still very much in demand in an integrative approach, in which existing protection concepts and also hazard mitigation measures, such as structural measures against floods, should not be completely shelved. Instead, these should be linked more with an equally strong emphasis on the impact chains and the vulnerability of society as well as infrastructure. This is also understood as integrated risk management. Resilience is sometimes de facto simply superimposed as a new term on the previous risk term (S. L. Cutter et al., 2008) and thus, similar to hazard prevention terms in civil protection, comprehensively describes all types of organisational and technical, structural and non-structural measures. Sometimes resilience is also subsumed under what had previously been developed in social ecological systems or complexity theory: a combination of non-linear processes, with stochastic components and emergence of new states that were not foreseen before, close couplings and interdependencies (Lewin, 1992; Waldrop, 1992).

With this new understanding, cities and municipalities can, on the one hand, adapt to a new form of management, not only in hazard prevention. Instead of protection and defence measures, it is now possible to argue in a broader and more integrative way and to establish more cooperation between departments. However, this poses new challenges for many municipalities, as this is usually not included in the typical administrative structures and ways of thinking. Here, according to a further development of the organisational structures, resilience development can be promoted. Likewise, people are now needed who possess such competences in order to be able and allowed to think and work in an interdisciplinary manner. This can be done through further education and training as well as coaching and exchange in networks and platforms (CaDRI, 2011). However, there are many analogies to similar ways of thinking, for example in agile management or even in already established areas such as that in business continuity management. Here, too, the focus is on measures to respond to arbitrary crises with a lot of flexibility, as opposed to rigid hierarchical structures.

However, there are other measures that cities and municipalities can use to prepare for crises. Here it is not so important whether this is called resilience or risk. After all, the new German resilience strategy of the Ministry of the Interior also contains, in principle, many components from the 2015 Sendai Framework for Disaster Reduction (Die Bundesregierung, 2022). Thus, current thoughts on a risk-informed society with many components of risk analysis and risk management go hand in hand with ideas of smarter reconstruction after disasters (build back better) and a general understanding of resilience in many subject areas (United Nations, 2015). This also includes a better understanding of risks, which is important, for example, through better information procurement and thus also monitoring for cities and municipalities, not only in the case of floods, forest fires, pandemics and also civil protection requirements such as energy shortages. In the flood of 2021, the need for digital situation maps, warnings and other information bases became very clear in many regions (Fekete & Sandholz, 2021). In order to do justice to the core idea of resilience, hitherto unknown or unusual hazards must be addressed in order to avoid a "lock-in", i.e. persisting in old patterns of thinking and behaviour (Pendall et al., 2010). Climate change is already making it clear that new types of hazards as well as already known hazards must be taken into account with a new intensity and frequency in order to make societies fit for the future. Another goal called for in the resilience strategy as well as in the Sendai Framework is better cooperation between a wide range of actors, within a municipality but also between municipalities and their neighbouring countries. Institutions also need to be strengthened, as does the business community, which needs to get more involved. After all, more than 80 % of the so-called critical infrastructure is in private hands and thus a great responsibility lies with municipalities as well as with the economy and the operators of such infrastructures (BMI, 2009).

Cities and municipalities can also be better prepared for crises if they combine new tasks such as the transformation towards more sustainability with crisis resistance. Reconstruction in regions affected by floods or forest fires can at the same time reduce energy consumption in the longer term or, by creating more shelter for the environment, simultaneously lead to a sponge city capability where floods and heavy rains are used to simultaneously create water storage for dry summers and hot spells. To this end, a number of scientists have already proposed five-point plans for the transformation of municipalities (Kuhlicke et al., 2021). Besides the physical-technical transformation of urban spaces, developments at the societal level can also contribute to strengthening crisis resilience. Social and economic factors such as educational opportunities, employment and income, health care, participation opportunities or access to public services thus increase the resilience of individuals and become drivers of societal resilience (S. Cutter, L., Burton, & Emrich, 2010).

3. Aspects of appropriate crisis management

A self-understanding of one's own importance as an actor and enabling various actors to develop competencies independently and to network is a good start for appropriate municipal crisis management. Crises affect a municipality comprehensively in many different fields and therefore require an independent capacity to act in many individual fields, as well as the cross-sectoral cooperation already mentioned. This also requires an overall understanding of the system, which municipalities often have to create first. In crises with supply chain dependencies, for example, the pandemic or the blockade of the Suez Canal made it very clear how vulnerable the current supply of essential goods, as well as goods necessary for the economy, has become. Authorities and industry often lack simple overviews of the networks with suppliers and the dependencies they have created themselves. For this purpose, an actor mapping is necessary that shows the actors involved in the municipality and outside. Subsequently, a dependency analysis is carried out to reveal possible Achilles heels for the functioning of the individual companies and to gain an impression of potential impact chains across company and sector boundaries. As a measure, an organisational concept is then recommended which, in addition to the network and the interconnections of dependencies, also lists contact persons and alternatives that can be addressed as redundancy in an emergency. In the case of particularly sensitive critical infrastructures in the municipal sector, such as in health care, emergency plans must be drawn up that prepare the basic supply of water, electricity and information for various scenarios. In this preparation, however, it must also be taken into account when independent or supported emergency care is no longer possible and consequently an evacuation becomes necessary in order to avoid or reduce personal injury.

It is also important for 'good' crisis management to integrate both different actors and in the mindset of different phases of action, before, during and after a crisis. However, it is important to dovetail competences instead of continuing to maintain a pigeonhole thinking and to consider responsibilities separately.

Specialisation and division of labour is necessary for everyday efficiency issues, but in the event of a crisis it is sometimes a hindrance. Clear responsibilities and also the preparation of hierarchical management organisations such as staffs must continue to be maintained and practised on the one hand, also in the cooperation of different staffs and municipal actors. For example, a better link between risk management as an area of responsibility in planning and preparation before a crisis and crisis management from the moment of a crisis is necessary, to be practised and also financially supported.

Above all, however, the user perspective of the population must not be forgotten. Participation processes certainly have their limits, especially when it comes to disaster preparedness, but the overall understanding at the municipal level is still far too strongly characterised by top-down structures. Trust is placed in the hands of many volunteers and honorary staff, especially outside the big cities. In cities, on the other hand, much more of the municipalities' own responsibility and ability to act is handed over to the professional fire brigade and others. In the case of major crises and disasters, however, the limits quickly become clear, as was the case most recently with the floods of 2021. Therefore, an early involvement of the population in preparedness and training as well as information processing is necessary and also possible as participation in research projects, for example. Here, too, it becomes apparent that an increase in the willingness to act at the individual and organisational level strengthens society's ability to deal with crises. However, individuals must by no means be left to their own devices; rather, it is necessary to offer cooperation on an equal footing, provide information and support, as well as a willingness for mutual learning between the municipality and its citizens. It is also important to consider how good crisis management can better involve volunteers and spontaneous helpers in municipal work from the outset and also in disaster management with staff work. There are many guidelines and lessons learned documents on crisis management from the studies of the 2021 flood alone.

Universities and research institutions can support municipalities very well in the transfer of knowledge and competence between practice and science and back. Opportunities are available for jointly funded third-party projects, in which, for example, concepts for resilience for minimum supply in the event of a disaster for the failure of critical infrastructure such as electricity, water or heat have already been implemented in some regions (Fekete, Neisser, Tzavella, & Hetkämper, 2019). In addition to the effect of professional exchange on concrete methods and measures for action, such joint research projects between science and practice, but also joint workshops and conferences, above all create important networks and contacts. In this way, cross-municipal projects in particular can help some actors in emergency response to get together with operators of critical infrastructure and municipal administrations on such topics, often for the first time ever.

3. 1 Civil protection and infrastructure

The issue of power outages and increasingly water shortages, but also the energy shortage due to the Ukraine war as well as attacks on railways or pipelines have once again highlighted the need to address the issue of critical infrastructure. Likewise, many municipalities are not only increasingly threatened by cyber attacks, but have actually already had to experience them.

An important first measure for action is to first identify the particularly important and thus critical infrastructures at the municipal level. To this end, civil protection authorities have already developed guidelines that enable municipalities to identify critical infrastructures on their own (BBK, 2017). There are also training courses and advanced training at the German federal academy BABZ (Bundesakademie für Bevölkerungsschutz und Zivile Verteidigung - Federal Academy for Civil Protection and Civil Defence). Finally, research projects are another way to carry out this cooperation with universities and often it is already possible to promote junior staff and enable them to work in the municipalities later on.

After a spatial identification of critical infrastructure, it is also possible to make this information available and visualise it for many departments, for example in the form of geographical information systems. It should be noted here, however, that in the case of particularly sensitive object types, it should be checked whether information about them should also be made public or should remain in the protected area. This is because failures due to sabotage must also be considered seriously and possible hostile actors should not be offered any opportunities for attack. However, a good information base is essential for repairing everyday damage caused by digging accidents or the like, and is also very important for the expansion of broadband and basic services. Likewise, one must then already be prepared for emergencies or disasters, in case one or more particularly important infrastructures fail and, for example, people have to be evacuated from hospitals and accommodated and cared for elsewhere. Bomb finds from the Second World War also cause some municipalities to have to carry out such temporary evacuations again and again.

Based on current research, it is also advisable to consider minimal supply concepts that can still guarantee minimal functionality in particularly severe crises in the understanding of resilience. In other words, infrastructures and also competencies and resources in the municipality must be identified that need to be particularly protected and prioritised so that they can help to supply others in a crisis and to prepare and accompany the reconstruction of functional capability. This includes emergency power concepts and grid replacement systems, as well as refuelling concepts and food reserves, as well as island capabilities of telecommunications and possibly also power and energy supply.

In addition to these aspects, modern civil protection must also deal with the possibility of simultaneous hazards, for example if a flood occurs in addition to a pandemic. Likewise, interdependencies of infrastructures and possible cascading effects must be planned for, if, for example, many other infrastructures can fail due to the failure of the power supply.

The identification of such interdependencies and cascading effects between different actors can be facilitated mainly through round tables or discussion groups. To start with, no complex staff framework exercises are necessary here, but a basic exchange about understandings of responsibilities and competences. To support this, or as a next step, a discussion of hypothetical scenarios can take place. Possible guiding questions can be:

- What happens to my system?
- Which specific infrastructures or services fail?
- Who depends on these infrastructures/services?
- How can these infrastructures/services be maintained or what redundancies/back-up levels are available?
- How can I reach other actors (also at night or on Sundays and public holidays) and who is the contact person?

These round tables can also be specialised for different tasks or areas to enable exchange at technical and organisational levels.

It is important to understand that for cross-organisational resilient risk and crisis management, basic factors and conditions must be met. This can be illustrated as in Figure 1.

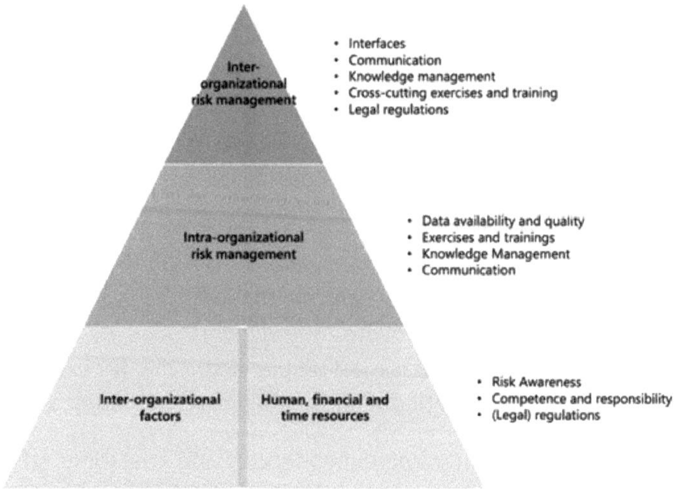

Figure 1: Hierarchy of necessary factors for integrated risk management (Own representation).

First of all, there must be sufficient human, financial and time resources as well as other factors internal to the organisation, such as a proper awareness of responsibility and risk. On this basis, an organisation-internal risk management can be built up. The aim here is not to achieve a perfect system immediately, but to strive for constant improvement, similar to business continuity management or quality management. When there is finally a system with which an organisation has created the conditions internally to deal with risks and crises in a structured way, external actors can be involved and a cross-organisational risk management can be established.

There, communication with each other and with the population is particularly important in order to maintain a functioning system. Due to its great importance, this topic is dealt with in the following section.

3. 2 Crisis communication and legitimacy in crisis mode

What constitutes good, appropriate communication in crisis mode? What should be considered here and what goals should be pursued?

Successful crisis communication is a central part of crisis management and essential for successfully managing a crisis (BMI, 2014). In crises, great expectations are placed on municipalities in terms of warning and information from the official side. Digitalisation has increased the expectations even more, and rapid and reliable communication is expected at a faster pace than before. In addition to the speed and official character, the otherwise usual principles of good communication must also be observed, which can be easily read in guidelines at the Federal Office of Civil Protection and Disaster Assistance, for example (BMI, 2014).

However, the strong influence of social media on the current media landscape also places formal demands on crisis communication: In order to be seen on common social media platforms, reporting must follow the rules that apply there. This means not only the provision of content and information in real time, but also in particular the use of image and video material and the formulation of catchy messages in order to attract the attention of users in the first place (Bachmann & Ternès von Hattburg, 2021; Nolting & Thießen, 2008).

However, the floods of 2021 and the COVID-19 pandemic have highlighted special requirements for public relations and warnings. In addition to the pure dissemination of information, the two-way practice must also be strengthened so that citizens have an immediate point of contact in the event of a crisis, not only to receive information but also to be able to reflect it back. This can save an enormous amount of time in a crisis and save people if those affected and involved can use their smartphones or other means not only to make emergency calls, but also to send instructions for rescue operations.

For good communication, it is also necessary to optimise the organisation of communication. This also means that staff work should be more concerned with public relations and press work than in the past, and that communication with other actors in the community should be established permanently and from the outset. For example, access to information in the situation must be better shared with the municipalities, and care must also be taken to ensure that communication ladders up and down the hierarchical structures through the higher administrative units do not lead to a loss of time. Thus, cross-border cooperation between neighbouring municipalities under different district affiliations, for example, has been a problem so far. But the integration of local expertise into staff work in major disaster situations is also necessary.

As an example, it is already planned before crises whether and which liaison persons will be sent to other staffs in order to enable a direct exchange of information and expertise. The German Federal Agency for Technical Relief (THW), for example, has built up a broad network of expert advisors in Germany to inform and advise crisis teams about THW's options for action. But in order to make use of this service, it should be known in advance how to access such resources.

For municipalities, a close exchange with basic suppliers for energy and drinking water, for example, is relevant, but the importance of medical and civil protection infrastructure must not be neglected either. In the context of a blackout scenario, the following questions, among others, must be considered:

- Are local hospitals still functional?
- How long will fuel supplies last? In addition to buildings supplied with emergency power, this also concerns the emergency vehicles of the fire brigade and rescue service and should not be neglected under any circumstances.
- Is the hospital facing a critical decision of evacuation or clearance? If so, sufficient lead time for planning and execution must be considered.
- What are the channels of communication?
- What should be done if communication channels fail (telephone, internet, mobile phone, etc.)?

Finally, the technical possibilities for communication must also be improved; the use of digital radio in particular has been a problematic issue in civil protection for many years, as has the use of text-based messages (cell broadcasting) or other technical possibilities, which are not yet fully exploited in Germany compared to other countries. For the Warning Day in December 2022, the function of cell broadcasting was now tested for the first time in Germany in order to be able to use it in the future. And in addition to crisis communication, preparation and precaution through risk communication must also be taken into account (BBK, 2022).

Consequently, it can be seen that strong municipal resilience consists of the building blocks of effective and efficient risk and crisis management. In a holistic and integrated approach, different actors need to be involved in order to identify interdependencies. In addition, the civilian population - a major component of a community - should not be neglected. The best preparation of authorities and organisations is useless if the population is not warned in crises, does not know how to act or does not know any contact points for emergencies or further information.

3. 3 Communication with the participation of the population and the acceptance of political decisions by the population

Due to digitalisation and social media, but also due to a changed self-image of society, more and more forms of participation in communication are expected. However, the problems of participation formats are often not yet sufficiently discussed in public. With regard to democratic participation, two problems arise here. On the one hand, it can happen that people reject the responsibility for dealing with a crisis and do not take advantage of their opportunity for democratic participation. On the other hand, it can happen in the opposite way that decisions are made and communicated by the political side, but these do not find acceptance among the population.

Especially when it comes to crises and disasters, many people understandably have fears of contact or, especially in emergencies, think that responsibility should lie with the organisations set up for this purpose. Participation must therefore not only be made possible, but often it must first be advertised. And if one promises participation, one must also ensure that it is real participation and that success can also occur if one participates (Arnstein, 1969). Although these principles from participation research have been known since the 1960s, they are less widespread in Germany than in some other neighbouring countries, especially in the very hierarchically structured disaster management of the municipalities, also due to the established organisations. Conversely, this also leads to a certain passivity in disaster preparedness and in the ability of people in a municipality to act. Not only the authorities and organisations with security tasks must be aware of their responsibility, but also the population for self-protection and self-sufficiency.

On the other hand, social media in particular have also revealed new problems when certain groups of people seek out online forums that reinforce their own opinions and form a kind of echo chamber in which one finds mainly like-minded opinions. This can then become a problem if these are radicalising opinions or those that also spread anti-democratic opinions or conspiracy theories. At the local level, it is important to be aware of how strong a link there can be to political opinion-making and thus a proximity to local politics. In principle, social media and their echo chambers are an extension of the regulars' table and must be taken into account when communicating about crises. Because otherwise, in addition to a crisis, the self-reinforcing effects of social discontent are added, which in the case of an escalation of a crisis can quickly also end up in the obstruction of emergency forces or in the acceptance of collective measures and in the blocking of the finding of a social consensus. On the other hand, freedom of opinion and critical debate are equally indispensable in a community and must therefore continue to be promoted and integrated. Thus, integrative thinking and a cross-sectoral mindset is already important here and it is advisable to cover the population as broadly as possible in an inclusive approach at an early stage and in the participation of the most diverse social groups.

Both challenges described make the relevance of comprehensive risk communication clear. In contrast to crisis communication, this is not carried out in relation to an acute situation, but continuously in order to inform citizens about risks in general and to enable them to make risk-conscious decisions and lifestyles (BMI 2014). This is also a measure for capacity development at the individual level. The risk literacy thus created can enable the population to be more responsible and willing to participate. Since the broader society often has a distorted understanding of risk, which is caused not least by disproportionate reporting, effective risk communication is particularly important to create a basic understanding of risks and to leave misinformation less of an influence (Nolting 2008). Realistic expectations also include the realisation that risk communication alone cannot prevent the emergence of societal conflicts, as different values and needs continue to lead to different opinions about risks and countermeasures (National Research Council, 1989). However, good risk communication can strengthen the public's trust in the communicating institutions and reputable sources and thus prevent the spread of conspiracy myths in crisis situations.

4. Conclusion and outlook

In summary, municipalities need the appropriate competencies of their staff for future crises, including the ability to think, plan and act across sectors. In addition, there must also be specialists who can deal with issues in depth and independently, even across changes of government. Both types of competence together also require a crisis management culture that promotes this broad and specialised thinking at the same time. This also includes an openness to constantly adapt to new crises and even overlaps of crises and to live with change. Strengthening the resilience of the organisation also still requires a suitable form of coordination and communication that combines both participation formats and clearly regulated structures. Technical aspects of all kinds also contribute to the resilience of, among other things, critical infrastructure and basic services, which have become indispensable in everyday life as well as especially in the event of a crisis.

Disaster preparedness as well as crisis management can lead to resilience, where not everything is predictable and damage as well as negative experiences occur, but one goes through a crisis together as a community and does not break apart as a community or municipality in the end. Analogous to the coat of arms of Paris, a commune may fluctuate and remain in flux and change, but not perish through cohesion despite disputes.

Literature

Arnstein, S. R. (1969). A ladder of citizen participation. Journal of the American Institute of planners, 35(4), 216-224.

Bachmann, S., & Ternès von Hattburg, A. (2021). Virtuelle Meetings–digital effektiv kommunizieren. In Effiziente Krisenkommunikation–transparent und authentisch (pp. 17-21): Springer.

BBK. (2017). Schutz Kritischer Infrastrukturen – Identifizierung in sieben Schritten. Arbeitshilfe für die Anwendung im Bevölkerungsschutz. Retrieved from Bonn, Germany:

BBK. (2022). Risikokommunikation. Ein Handbuch für die Praxis. Retrieved from Bonn:

Becker, P. (2014). Sustainability science: Managing risk and resilience for sustainable development. Waltham, MA, USA: Elsevier.

Bergström, J., & Dekker, S. W. (2014). Bridging the macro and the micro by considering the meso: reflections on the fractal nature of resilience. Ecology and Society, 19(4).

BMI. (2009). Nationale Strategie zum Schutz Kritischer Infrastrukturen (KRITIS-Strategie). Berlin: Bundesministerium des Innern.

BMI. (2014). Leitfaden Krisenkommunikation. Berlin: Bundesministerium des Innern.

Bogardi, J. J., & Fekete, A. (2018). Disaster-Related Resilience as Ability and Process: a concept guiding the analysis of response behavior before, during and after extreme events. American Journal of Climate Change, 7, 54-78.

CaDRI. (2011). Basics of capacity development for disaster risk reduction. In: Capacity for Disaster Reduction Initiative Geneva, Switzerland.

Coaffee, J., & Lee, P. (2017). Urban resilience: Bloomsbury Publishing.

Cutter, S., L., Burton, C., G., & Emrich, C., T. (2010). Disaster Resilience Indicators for Benchmarking Baseline Conditions. In Journal of Homeland Security and Emergency Management (Vol. 7).

Cutter, S. L., Barnes, L., Berry, M., Burton, C., Evans, E., Tate, E., & Webb, J. (2008). A place-based model for understanding community resilience. Global Environmental Change, 18, 598–606.

Die Bundesregierung. (2022). Deutsche Strategie zur Stärkung der Resilienz gegenüber Katastrophen. Umsetzung des Sendai Rahmenwerks für Katastrophenvorsorge (2015–2030) – Der Beitrag Deutschlands 2022–2030. Retrieved from Berlin:

Fekete, A. (2022). Kritische Infrastruktur und Versorgung der Bevölkerung: Springer.

Fekete, A., Neisser, F., Tzavella, K., & Hetkämper, C. (Eds.). (2019). Wege zu einem Mindestversorgungskonzept. Kritische Infrastrukturen und Resilienz. Cologne, Germany: TH Köln.

Fekete, A., & Rhyner, J. (2020). Sustainable digital transformation of disaster risk—integrating new types of digital social vulnerability and interdependencies with critical infrastructure. Sustainability, 12(22), 9324.

Fekete, A., & Sandholz, S. (2021). Here Comes the Flood, but Not Failure? Lessons to Learn after the Heavy Rain and Pluvial Floods in Germany 2021. Water, 13(21), 3016. Retrieved from https://www.mdpi.com/2073-4441/13/21/3016

Gunderson, L. H., & Holling, C. S. (2002). Panarchy. Understanding Transformations in Human and Natural Systems. Washington: Island Press.

Hagelsteen, M., & Burke, J. (2016). Practical aspects of capacity development in the context of disaster risk reduction. International Journal of Disaster Risk Reduction, 16, 43-52. doi:https://doi.org/10.1016/j.ijdrr.2016.01.010

Heylighen, F., Cilliers, P., & Gershenson, C. (2006). Complexity and philosophy. arXiv preprint cs/0604072.

Holling, C. S. (1973). Resilience and Stability of Ecological Systems. Annual Review of Ecology and Systematics, 4, 1-23. Retrieved from www.jstor.org

Kuhlicke, C., Albert, C., Bachmann, D., Birkmann, J., Borchardt, D., Fekete, A., . . . Voss, M. (2021). Fünf Prinzipien für klimasichere Kommunen und Städte. Five principles for climate-proof municipalities and cities. Retrieved from Leipzig, Germany: https://www.ufz.de/index.php?en=48382

Lewin, R. (1992). Complexity: Life at the Edge of Chaos. Chicago The University of Chicago Press.

National Research Council. (1989). Improving risk communication. Washington (DC), USA: National Academies Press.

Nolting, T., & Thießen, A. (2008). Krisenmanagement in der Mediengesellschaft. In Krisenmanagement in der Mediengesellschaft (pp. 9-18): Springer.

Norris, F. H., Stevens, S. P., Pfefferbaum, B., Wyche, K. F., & Pfefferbaum, R. L. (2008). Community resilience as a metaphor, theory, set of capacities, and strategy for disaster readiness. American journal of community psychology, 41(1), 127-150.

Pelling, M. (2003). The Vulnerability of Cities: Natural Disasters and Social Resilience: Routledge.

Pelling, M. (2010). Adaptation to climate change: from resilience to

transformation: Routledge.
Pendall, R., Foster, K. A., & Cowell, M. (2010). Resilience and regions: building understanding of the metaphor. Cambridge Journal of Regions, Economy and Society, 3(1), 71-84. doi:10.1093/cjres/rsp028
Schulz, K., Gustafsson, I., & Illes, E. (2005). Manual for capacity development. Stockholm: Sida.
Tobin, G. A. (1999). Sustainability and community resilience: the holy grail of hazards planning? Global Environmental Change Part B: Environmental Hazards, 1(1), 13-25.
UN/ISDR. (2005). Hyogo Framework for Action 2005-2015: Building the resilience of nations and communities to disasters (HFA). Retrieved from Geneva:
UNDRR. (2022). Terminology. Retrieved from https://www.undrr.org/terminology
United Nations. (2015). Sendai Framework for Disaster Risk Reduction 2015 – 2030. Retrieved from United Nations Office for Disaster Risk Reduction: Geneva, Switzerland:
Waldrop, M. M. (1992). Complexity. The emerging science at the edge of order and chaos. London: Edition of 1994, Penguin Books.

For further elaboration

- German strategy to strengthen resilience to disasters https://www.bbk.bund.de/DE/Themen/Nationale-Kontaktstelle-Sendai-Rahmenwerk/Resilienzstrategie/resilienz-strategie_node.html
- Information of the Federal Government, the Federal Office of Civil Protection and Disaster Assistance on Critical Infrastructures
- www.kritis.bund.de
- Sendai Framework
- https://www.bbk.bund.de/SharedDocs/Downloads/DE/Fremd-Publikationen/SENDAI/sendai-rahmenwerk-2015-2030.pdf?__blob=publicationFile&v=4
- Federal Academy for Civil Protection and Civil Defence
- https://www.bbk.bund.de/DE/Themen/Akademie-BABZ/akademie-babz_node.html
- Wamsler, Christine. Cities, disaster risk and adaptation. 1st ed. London: Routledge, 2014. https://doi.org/10.4324/9780203486771.

- Shaw, R., M. Colley, and R. Connell. "Climate Change Adaptation by Design: A Guide for Sustainable Communities." London: TCPA, 2007.https://www.preventionweb.net/files/7780_20070523CCA-lowres1.pdf.
- Media Library https://www.bbk.bund.de/SiteGlobals/Forms/Suche/Mediathek/Mediathek_Formular.html?nn=21806

Lectures

Andrew B. Wootton, Caroline L. Davey, Dagmar P. Heinrich, Francesc Guillén Lasierra

The perception, impact and handling of feelings of insecurity

1. Abstract

Outbreaks of feelings of insecurity may result in citizens openly protesting that they feel unsafe — for example, through public demonstrations, public meetings or on social media. Public authorities might assume the problem facing citizens is one of actual crime victimisation. However, factors influencing perceptions of insecurity may have little or nothing to do with the experience of crime victimisation.

Policymakers and practitioners need to better understand and address factors impacting citizens' feelings of insecurity. Interventions should be based on a systematic understanding of insecurity causal factors. An ill-considered response that is insensitive to the problem context, has the potential to not only fail to solve the problem, but may even make it worse.

To support practitioners and security policymakers in better understanding and addressing citizens' feelings of insecurity, the Cutting Crime Impact (CCI) project developed the CCI Feelings of Unsafety Lifecycle model as a conceptual framework. CCI supported six European law enforcement agencies in conducting research to understand the breadth of contextual factors impacting and influencing citizens' feelings of insecurity. This led to the development of solutions tailored to their specific context to help end-users identify the responses required, and support the process of planning and taking action.

This chapter focuses on work conducted in collaboration with the Department of the Interior in Catalonia (ES) to understand and address citizens' feelings of insecurity. The Department of Interior developed a guide to analysing and responding to outbreaks of insecurity – "Perception Matters" – available in Catalan, Spanish and English. Section 1 of the guide contains the CCI Feelings of Unsafety Lifecycle Model.

2. The issue – feelings of insecurity

Feelings of insecurity may impact citizens' behaviour and use of civic amenities with, for example, parks or public transport facilities being underused or avoided. Outbreaks of feelings of insecurity may manifest in concerned citizens publicly protesting their safety concerns, for example, by expressing disapproval via traditional print and social media, speaking out at public meetings or organising public demonstrations. At this point, however, understanding of the factors underlying their feelings of insecurity will only be superficial. Effort is required to gain useful insight that can support appropriate action.

3. Actions for impacting insecurity

The following actions are required to understand and effectively mitigate citizens' feelings of insecurity:

3. 1 Policymakers and practitioners need to understand the factors causing feelings of insecurity

Practitioners should not assume insecurity to be only related to crime victimisation. Other causal factors may be responsible. For example, anxiety can result from the nature and quality of a person's immediate environment. Feelings of anxiety may be fostered by, for example, poor-quality street lighting or visible evidence of antisocial behaviour (e.g. litter, graffiti, broken windows, vandalised street furniture, and so on). Citizens may come to avoid such environments, contributing to a potential downward spiral of underuse and raised anxiety levels amongst other potential users.

Anxiety can arise from the prospect of being or feeling vulnerable. Feelings of insecurity may be caused by citizens' assumptions about future vulnerability. The individual feels anxious at the prospect of being in a particular situation — for example, when considering walking home late at night. The person may take precautionary measures in response to their perceived vulnerability — or might change their behaviour. For example, instead of walking, take the car. In such cases, simply improving the design of public amenities may not be enough, measures that seek to actively change citizens' attitudes, perceptions or behaviours will be required.

3. 2 Policymakers and practitioners should seek a systematic understanding of feelings of insecurity and make use of effective conceptual models

Conceptual models are required that operationalise the different elements that constitute feelings of insecurity to support policymakers and practitioners in understanding, measuring and addressing citizens' feelings of insecurity. The Cutting Crime Impact (CCI) project developed the Feelings of Unsafety Lifecycle Model (see Figure 1) as a conceptual framework to support security practitioners and policymakers. The model includes the stages in the cycle of unsafety — from assumptions made prior to being in a situation, through experience of a situation (including possible crime victimisation), to rationalisation of that experience and sharing this with family, friends and neighbours. Terminology should be precise, with terms like 'fear' only being used in its correct context, such as when a citizen is being threatened or victimised — the more common negative experience being 'worry' or 'anxiety'.

3. 3 Policymakers and practitioners need to prevent and mitigate the impact of victimisation

Experience of victimisation can foster feelings of insecurity, with the victim feeling more vulnerable in particular locations or contexts. This may give rise to avoidance strategies or, in extreme cases, complete lifestyle changes. For example, an individual victimised at a bus stop may begin avoiding public transport. Such responses to victimisation can seriously inhibit an individual's quality of life, limiting their use of local amenities and services and reducing participation in their community.

Over the longer term, a victim must psychologically process their experience — perhaps discussing the incident with family, friends or neighbours. This sharing of experience can result in a relatively local shared perspective regarding risk of victimisation, reinforcing shared anxieties.

Growth in the use of social media has greatly increased the ability of experiences and opinions to be shared very quickly, extremely widely, and often anonymously. Negative and sensationalist stories are known to be 'sticky', in that they are more likely to be shared and remembered than positive ones. A constant background noise of negative stories can skew perceptions.

The quality of support a citizen receives post-victimisation (whether victim support services, prevention advice or social media groups) can mitigate the negative consequences for the individual. This will in turn impact the 'story' shared by the individual with their immediate family and friends, and so may interrupt the cycle of feelings of unsafety.

3. 4 Tools should provide a finer grain understanding of the experience of unsafety and how this impacts citizen beliefs and behaviour

Traditionally, policymakers and practitioners have relied on victimisation surveys to gain insight into citizens' feelings of insecurity. However, focusing on crime victimisation neglects the broader context of feelings of unsafety – often involving factors unconnected with victimisation.

Qualitative tools that seek to understand citizen behaviours in response to feelings of unsafety[1] can provide alternative strategies for tackling them and provide solutions suited to the specific context.

4. The CCI Feelings of Unsafety Lifecycle model

The term 'feelings of insecurity' is vague and too easily misunderstood or misapplied to be useful. The authors suggest a better, more precise term would be *Feelings of Unsafety*. Conceptually, this is where the CCI *Feelings of Unsafety Lifecycle Model* begins — a model developed originally in 2014 by Davey and Wootton, and adapted for use in the CCI project (see **Figure 1**).

1 For example, the LKA INSIGHT Tool, which can be found here: https://www.cuttingcrimeimpact.eu/toolkits/insight/lka---/

The first part of the Feelings of Unsafety model is "*Assumed Situational Vulnerability*". This is 'Contextualised anxiety' — that is, anxiety about a location or activity, based on assumptions. Consequently, it is felt before a person is actually in a situation. For example, someone feeling anxious about visiting a location before they actually leave the house.

The next stage in the model is "*Situational Anxiety*". This relates to feelings of unsafety or anxiety experienced when present in a particular context or environment. For example, this is feeling anxious when walking alone through a poorly-lit public space at night.

The authors reserve use of the term "*fear*" for the stage immediately preceding the person becoming a victim of crime.

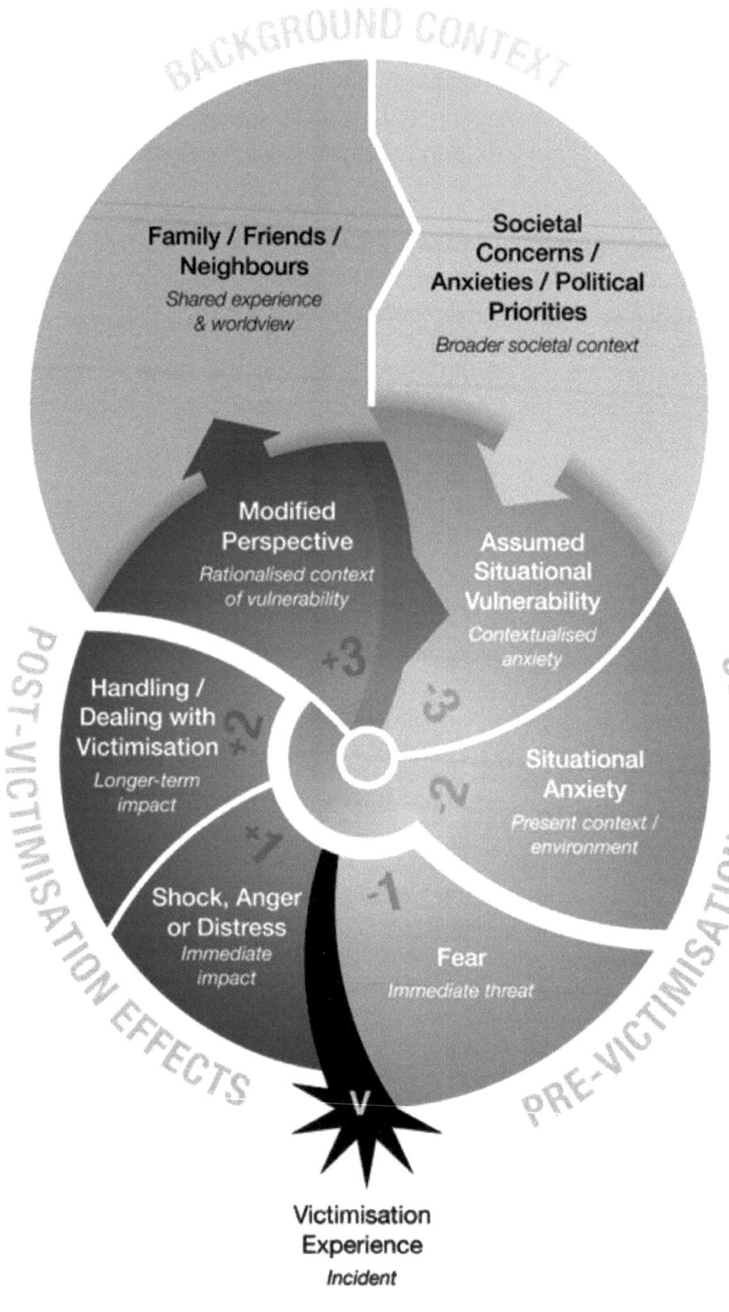

Figure 1. The Feelings of Unsafety Lifecycle Model

This is the sense of 'immediate threat' felt just prior to a crime incident — before the victimisation event — be that robbery, assault, or other personal crime type. Victimisation is followed by the *"Shock, Anger or Distress"* stage of the model. This is the immediate impact of the crime incident on the victim and, importantly, on the offender. This is followed by what the authors term *"Handling or Dealing with Victimisation"* — the longer-term impact of the experience of victimisation on the individual. This in turn results in a modification of the person's perspective — what the authors term their *"Rationalised context of vulnerability"*. This may be the result of an internal dialogue rationalising events, for example:

> *"I walked through that location, which I previously thought was safe, but because of my negative experience [or their victimisation], I now realise that I am not safe in that location — I am vulnerable in that location".*

The *Feelings of Unsafety Lifecycle Model* includes stages relating to 'Pre-Victimisation Factors' and to what the authors term 'Post-Victimisation Effects'. These stages are numbered with respect to their distance from the 'Victimisation Experience' — that is, 'minus three' through to 'plus three'. Of course, an individual does not need to be victimised to have their negative feelings of unsafety reinforced. It is perfectly possible for a person to move from stage minus two, *"Situational Anxiety"*, to stage plus three, *"Modified Perspective"*. For example, "*Situational Anxiety*" in an environment that is badly designed or poorly managed and maintained may cause a person to negatively 'modify their perspective' regarding that location. Basically, their experience of the location was worse than they expected it to be, leading them to modify their assumptions regarding risk of victimisation. In this respect, the Model distinguishes the stages in which feelings of unsafety specifically relate to the experience of crime victimisation.

As the name suggests, the model represents a 'lifecycle' — as the modified perspective at stage plus three feeds into "*Assumptions of Situational Vulnerability*" made at stage minus three. Equally, such a *"Modified Perspective"* may inform the views of family, friends and neighbours when a person shares their experiences of unsafety (or victimisation), thereby creating a shared 'local worldview', which itself informs a broader societal context, shaping societal concerns, anxieties and, ultimately, political priorities. This "*Background Context*", communicated through traditional media and (increasingly) social media, also informs the "*Assumptions of Situational Vulnerability*" as constructed by the individual.

The authors suggest that the model represents a practical means of conceptualising "insecurity" or "feelings of unsafety", as at each stage of the model there exist positive and negative factors: ways of either increasing or reducing (making worse or making better) the impact of a particular stage on the citizen. The authors employed the model at a DesignLab workshop with CCI project partners to address four different real-world scenarios relating to citizens' feelings of unsafety in two of the LEA partners' cities — Hannover and Barcelona. The next section discusses one of the CCI Tools developed to address citizens' feelings of unsafety.

5. Example intervention in Catalonia

Outbreaks of perceptions of insecurity result in political pressure and require a rapid response that specifically targets causal factors. A common response is to rely on increased police presence and visibility — which generally doesn't tackle underlying problems. Such responses may result in a temporary cessation feelings of insecurity or of criminal activity. Often, however, a few weeks after the police raid, the local situation has reverted to its previous state.

As discussed, the reasons for feelings of insecurity can be various. The problem faced in Barcelona was groups of empty apartments being taken over by drug dealers and their customers. These are locally termed "*narcopisos*".

During the CCI project, the Department of Interior of Catalonia focused on the impact of 'narcopisos' on the feelings of insecurity of citizens living in one neighbourhood of Barcelona. While there was no recorded increase in actual victimisation rates, citizens perceived the risk of falling victim to crime as very high. In January 2020, residents took their displeasure to the streets and demonstrated against their perceived increasing insecurity. The Perception Matters Tool was developed from this research.

Perception Matters comprises a five-part manual that guides local practitioners step by step through the process of understanding and responding to outbreaks of perceptions of insecurity. The Tool outlines the ingredients of such an outbreak, how to decide on the immediacy of response required, how to analyse the situation and how to communicate the interventions and their progress to citizens.

The Perception Matters Tool was designed for use by those in charge of managing insecurity outbreaks — in general, prevention or governance services within the local administration. The Tool is suited to large municipalities that use prevention services or different security experts, and don't just rely on the police. The Tool may also be used by smaller municipalities that rely on senior police officers to plan and deliver a response that extends beyond the traditional police perspective.

Using Perception Matters, practitioners gained a better understanding of the situation. It became clear that communication between City Hall and local citizens was extremely poor. Consequently, residents were unaware of measures already taken by the city — or their positive impact on their neighbourhood. The Tool revealed that the problem stemmed from poor communication — rather than drug-related crime. Importantly, Catalonia now has a tool to better understand and effectively address any future problems of insecurity that emerge.

6. Discussion and conclusion

When seeking to understand the local safety context, in terms of sources of information there are the 'usual suspects' — that is crime statistics, conviction rates, arrest numbers and, potentially, data collected through public surveys. What is harder to assess is citizens' real perceptions of security — and the behaviours that these promote.

Generally, the traditional means for measuring feelings of insecurity has been the analysis of quantitative questions posed within victimisation surveys. Victimisation surveys typically measure insecurity using questions that begin, for example, "how worried are you about…". However, serious concerns have been raised about the questions related to so-called 'fear of crime'. Some studies accuse such surveys of actually constructing fear of crime as a significant social problem for a large proportion of the population (Farrell *et al.*, 2007).

Surveys also provide little insight into specific situations and scenarios related to feelings of insecurity (Buil-Gil *et al*, 2021). Criminological research shows that most factors influencing the perception of insecurity may have little or nothing to do with crime victimisation (Gray *et al*, 2008). Factors including unmanaged public space, the presence of perceived 'strangers', and a poorly maintained built environment may foster deep and persistent feelings of insecurity (Doran and Burgess, 2011; Guillén-Lasierra, 2021).

7. References

Buil-Gil, D., Moretti , A., Shlomo, N, and Medina, J. (2021) "Worry about crime in Europe: A model-based small area estimation from the European Social Survey". European Journal of Criminology. Vol 18(2), pp. 274-298

Davey, C.L., and Wootton, A.B. (2014) 'Crime and the Urban Environment: The Implications for Wellbeing' in Burton, R., Davies-Cooper,R. and Cooper, C. (Eds) Wellbeing. A Complete Reference Guide. Wiley-Blackwell: Chichester (UK)

Davey, C.L. and Wootton, A.B. (2017) Design Against Crime. A Human-Centred Approach to Designing for Safety and Security. Design for Socially Responsibility Series, (Ed) Professor Rachel Cooper, Routledge: Abingdon, Oxon.

Davey, C.L. and Wootton, A.B (2019) "Feelings of Insecurity Lifecycle model" in "PIM Toolkit 4: Report on feelings of insecurity – Concepts and models". Deliverable D7.2 EU-funded Cutting Crime Impact (CCI) project.

Doran, B.J. and Burgess, M.B. (2011) Putting Fear of Crime on the Map. Investigating Perceptions of Crime Using Geographic Information Systems. New York, Dordrecht, Heidelberg, London. Springer.

Gerber, M. M., Hirtenlehner, H., and Jackson, J. (2010). Insecurities about crime in Germany, Austria and Switzerland: A review of research findings. European Journal of Criminology, 7(2), 141-157.

Jackson, J., Farrell, S. D, and Gray, E. (2007) "Experience and Expression in the Fear of Crime: Full Research Report", ESRC End of Award Report, RES-000-23-1108. Swindon: ESRC. Available here.

Ferretti, F. Pozza, A. and Coluccia, A. (2018) "Urban safety: A re-reading of the sense of unsafety through individual and ecological dimensions", The European Journal of Criminology, pp. 1-22.

Gray, E. and Jackson, J. and Farrall, S. (2008) Reassessing the fear of crime. European journal of Criminology, 5 (3). pp. 363-380. ISSN

1477-3708.
Guillén-Lasierra, F. (2021). "The fallacy of objective security and its consequences". In International E-Journal of Criminal Sciences

8. Acknowledgements

The Cutting Crime Impact project received funding from the European Union's Horizon 2020 Research and Innovation programme under Grant Agreement No. 787100. The project ran from September 2018 to December 2021.

To find out more about the CCI project, visit www.CuttingCrimeImpact.eu.

For more information about measuring and mitigating citizens' feelings of insecurity in Catalonia, please contact Francesc Guillén, Department of Interior of the Generalitat of Catalonia, email: lapercepcioimporta@gencat.cat. Further details of the CCI Tool Perception Matters can be found at: www.cuttingcrimeimpact.eu/cci-toolkits/

Pilar De la Torre, Inès Amzal

Training local authorities to provide citizens with a safe urban environment by reducing the risks in public spaces

ABSTRACT

Local authorities play a key role in promoting and ensuring urban public spaces' security specifically through the lens of managing these public spaces. As public spaces are vital areas of urban life, they welcome all sorts of entertainment and actors and are therefore vulnerable to a wide range of risks and threats. From terrorism to panic movements and climate risks, the security of public spaces requires local actors to develop a common approach which would allow practitioners to be equipped with tools, methodologies and practices for dealing with safety issues affecting public spaces. The European Forum for Urban Security addressed these objectives in its manifesto "Security, democracy and cities : Co-producing urban security policies" released in 2021 which discussed the operations for securing public spaces in accordance with quality and social inclusion objectives. The project Secu4All developed in 2020 aimed at training local actors involved in the management of public spaces to provide citizens with a safe urban environment by reducing risks in public spaces through training on vulnerable assessment, crisis management communication and technologies for security in public spaces. This need for a common culture in terms of urban public spaces' security calls for a reflection on the diversity of risk and actors in public spaces but also on the skill-building of actors. The questions addressed are: How can the lack of common approach be solved? What can be done in order to enhance civic participation in the management of public spaces? How can one improve crisis communication strategies ? How can we evaluate monitoring and assessment tools to promote social cohesion ?

1. The European Forum for Urban Security's analysis on urban public spaces' security

A) Co-production of public space management: Efus' Approach

Efus' analysis on the management of public spaces is defined by the imperative of improving the security of such spaces while preserving their open and inclusive nature. Indeed, public spaces embody the intrinsic dynamism of urban life through their places dedicated to communication, gatherings, political demonstrations, artistic and cultural performances and all sorts of entertainment. However, these characteristics given to public spaces also makes them exposed to risks from incivilities, the presence of large crowds, to terrorism creating an increasing feeling of insecurity. Hence, the double positioning of Efus acknowledges the variety of risks and actors as well as the diversity of users and actors involved in running public spaces as factors to be incorporated in developing a management strategy for those spaces. In fact, these characteristics give public spaces a specific status in the domain of urban security: effectively, they require a security policy that is based on genuine cooperation between the different organisations and institutions concerned (local authorities, police, emergency services, user representatives…), for instance a co-production of security that guarantees that this type of urban place is both safe,open and accessible for everyone.

In order to achieve a real co-production of security in public spaces, it is essential to take into account multiple considerations such as the inclusion of minorities and those most vulnerable to becoming victims, as well as social inclusion objectives and the diverse use of public spaces according to the different times of the day and night. In this context, a holistic approach to capacity building for local actors involved in the management and protection of public spaces is recommended in Efus' approach to urban public spaces' security.

B) Contemplate the diversity of risks and actors in public spaces

Responsible for the design, management and protection of urban public spaces, local and regional authorities have to manage a wide range of actors from different disciplines, all with different skills and professional cultures. Although this type of partnership and cooperation is gaining ground at the local level, it is not yet the norm. However, it is a key factor for designing and managing public spaces where all citizens can feel not only safe and comfortable, but also listened to and involved in the decision-making.

As mentioned previously, the nature of public spaces are inherently complex which makes its security management attentive to all forms of incivility in public spaces and soft targets that have a tremendous impact on citizens' security and feelings of insecurity. Therefore, Efus' approach of security in public spaces is based on a holistic and multistakeholder perspective. This very approach allows cities to respond to the different risks and threats that may occur in public spaces. The promotion of a multistakeholder approach implies the coordination of local actors, including LEAs, city planners, civil society, organisations, private sector actors and communities which enables the mainstreaming of prevention, protection, reaction and anticipation elements in urban security policies to ensure safer public spaces that remain open, accessible and inclusive to all users.

Acknowledging and then involving the diversity of actors engaged in public spaces is not enough, it is also necessary to recognise the variety of risks existing in these spaces. The main security issues encountered in public spaces by local actors concern social or physical incivilities (vandalism, public drunkenness), the sharing of public spaces between different categories of the population or the difficulty of securing such spaces during large gatherings or events. Efus focuses on acts classified as crimes impacting public spaces as well as nuisances and incivilities.

Finally, addressing the variety of risks also involves a reflection on their different perceptions according to the population concerned. An analysis of fear levels according to the size of the city showed variations in triggers of fear. For example, people living in larger cities tended to be more fearful of crimes like terrorist attacks, especially if they had experienced such incidents in their city before. These issues can have an impact on social cohesion and increase citizens' and visitors' feeling of insecurity in relation to public spaces and therefore have to be in the overall strategy of public spaces management.

2. The Genesis and Implications of Secu4all

A) Secu4all insights

The Secu4all project is born out of the need to not only improve the capacity of local and regional authorities to develop coordinated actions but also to develop an efficient anticipation and preparedness for future threats. Secu4all aims to empower local and regional authorities with theoretical knowledge and practical tools to ensure the security of public spaces and the protection of soft targets (i.e. sports venues, shopping centres, schools,…) against potential threats. In this sense, specific training programmes were developed in the following four areas: vulnerability assessment, crisis communication, innovative technologies & urban planning.

As a way to implement a holistic approach, the project took into account the potential threat of terrorism as well as other crimes and possible forms of incivility in public spaces and soft targets that have a considerable impact on the security and feeling of insecurity of citizens. Through an integrated approach, the project allowed local actors to get familiar with the methods and tools available to identify, analyse and assess vulnerabilities in local public spaces as well as use innovative technologies to enhance the protection of these spaces while considering their ethical implications. Secu4all also proposes practices as far as crisis communication goes.

The project's objectives were intended to promote interactivity through training modules and field visits in addition to an e-learning platform with training content in Italian, German, English and French for greater reach and sustainability of the project's outcomes.

The consortium designed for this project also responded to the transversal aspiration of the project, therefore mixing local and regional authorities, organisations and academic partners and national forums. In this sense, Efus developed the Secu4all project on the basis of an exchange-based and didactic structure allowing a fulfillment of the engagements towards an efficient management of public spaces.

B) From knowledge development to knowledge dissemination

The Secu4All training consisted of 4 Modules. Each of them provided theoretical and practical knowledge so that the different actors involved in public spaces could contribute to their protection by ensuring their use by citizens who must feel safe and comfortable in these spaces:

- Module 1 - Vulnerability assessment
- Module 2 - Urban planning, design and management for urban security (UPDM-US)
- Module 3 - Crisis management communication
- Module 4 - Technologies for security in public spaces

Secu4All aimed at developing and increasing knowledge on the following basis :

1. **Knowledge development** with the creation of content and training material adapted to their needs (in practical terms) but with a solid theoretical foundation. The content was developed by the project partner organisations;
2. **Knowledge transfer** with the implementation of training courses delivered through virtual training sessions. Those sessions balanceda theoretical and practical outlook and included a significant number of local examples that participants could relate to
3. **Knowledge consolidation** with the organisation of 4 field visits which were organised within the framework of the project in order to consolidate the training contents and to provide concrete examples
4. **Knowledge dissemination**: Once the contents were tested, a training platform 'The Secu4All Padlet' was developed and this was free and easy to use in which all the contents and materials developed were uploaded. People who wished to follow the training could do so independently and could select topics of interest or follow each of the proposed modules. There they found readings, videos, podcasts, local examples and self-assessment and practical exercises.

3. Findings and challenges

A) Elaborating a common culture of the security of European public spaces: Training all stakeholders

As the security of public spaces constitutes a common challenge for everyone, it needs to be addressed through a common culture both in terms of the analysis of public spaces as a crossroads for several types of players as well as the requirement of a cross-training for the management of these spaces. In fact, all stakeholders should benefit from a co-production of security. In that sense, cities play a decisive role in promoting a shared culture of security issues in public spaces. In order to provide global and tailor-made solutions to public space issues, local security policies must include a common approach based on local and multistakeholder diagnosis. The creation of a collective knowledge will contribute to the general improvement of the local action concerning security practices. As a means to cultivate a common exercise of the security of European public spaces, the support for the skill-building of actors is necessary as it allows the improvement of local and regional authorities to develop coordinated actions and to be able to anticipate and prepare for future threats. An integrated approach as far as the assessment of vulnerabilities, crisis communication, the use of technologies and the reduction of citizens' feeling of insecurity are concerned should be implemented. The tools and methods mentioned are therefore the product of coordination and collaboration between the different actors and embody a platform to share good practices and lessons.

B) The importance of a vulnerability and risk assessment

Risk Assessment is an important part of the development of a security plan. Before one starts with the development of a security plan, it is important to understand the background of the environmental context in which any type of threat occurs. On the one hand, it is necessary to assess the attractiveness of the assets, places and events while, on the other hand, assess their vulnerability on the basis of the scenarios envisaged and the existing security/protective measures in place. Very well-known criminological theories on the social, psychological and physical environment of crime must be used. The risk assessment process is divided into three parts: risk identification, risk analysis and risk evaluation. The EU has developed tools to identify vulnerabilities in specific types of public spaces as well as a matrix according to which the level of risk can be calculated. The managing body that has carried out the vulnerability assessment needs to then define which risk is considered acceptable, and which is not. In a broader sense, conducting a vulnerability assessment and thus identifying gaps or vulnerabilities is especially valuable when municipalities or organisations are involved over the course of an event and have to ensure the security of a specific place. Conducting a vulnerability assessment, and thus identifying gaps or vulnerabilities, is particularly valuable when municipalities or any type of organisation is organising an event or has to ensure the security of a specific place.

C) Technology supporting the management of public spaces

The use of innovative technologies (drones, CCTV, biometric sensors, predictive policing tools, among others) by local security authorities is a reality. While it is true that their use is becoming increasingly common in European cities and other democratic contexts, it is no less true that as their use increases, so do the associated ethical, legal, and social issues. Due to the enormous conceptual and technical complexity of these topics, there is a significant risk of non-democratic uses of innovative technologies by local authorities directly affecting the civil rights and liberties of citizens. In the Secu4All project, it was a priority to interlink the dimensions of the legal fit, the ethical commitment and the positive social impact. In fact, any use of technological tools must be developed in accordance with the existing legal framework and comply with the relevant standards. With this in mind, the international, European, and national legal frameworks must be checked so that the development of the use of technological tools are consistent with these. Similarly, all technology must be used with respect for human, fundamental and civil rights. Finally, technology systems should not represent themselves as humans to users: humans have the right to be informed that they are interacting with an AI system. Hence, citizens should be involved in all phases of the development, implementation and use of technological systems for crime prevention through different strategies of popular consultation. This last concern touches on the challenge of citizen involvement as an essential part of the management strategy for public spaces.

D) Enhance citizen participation

Security is a complex issue that also relates to social aspects, such as cohesion, citizen participation and public resilience against any form of threat. Enhancing citizen participation embodies a challenge and aim of the Secu4all project. According to Efus, the use of art and culture should be increased to encourage citizen participation and improve the quality of public spaces. There are other strategies that are beneficial to their involvement. Adopting police tactics according to feelings of insecurity and improving the routine according to the citizens' needs seems to be a first step towards enhancing civic participation. Moreover, organising prevention groups that can meet on a regular basis (2 to 3 times a year) to analyse incivilities and identify public space resources embody citizens as actors with the capacity to be involved in the management of these spaces.

Closer ties between the police and inhabitants, and a better understanding of citizens' feelings of insecurity by the police can become a real vector for social cohesion and public safety. Training local authorities and training in schools helps to prepare future generations and to better integrate citizen participation in the measures implemented by cities in response to major crises to ensure their safety. It has become a requirement in order to work more effectively in partnership and foster the ability to anticipate, prevent and reduce the various types of risks and threats affecting public spaces.

It is important to note that participation can be defined differently from one actor to another, just as training may be conducted differently as stakeholders come from different cultures. This always has to be adjusted according to contexts and needs.

Lastly, citizens, when well-informed, can contribute to the overall strategy of public spaces' security through their expertise based on their day-to-day experience of these spaces. In order for this strategy to be efficient, citizens have to be not only involved in their local communities but also must have platforms available for them to exchange this information with local authorities.

Conclusion

The main challenge addressed by the Secu4All project is the training of local authorities to provide citizens with a safe urban environment by reducing the risks in public spaces,which in a broader sense implies a reflection on the political commitment of local communities to be involved in such a process. The practicality of the management of public spaces and their security demands tools and strategies based on a common approach allowing one to grasp the diversity and complexity of public spaces. Practices such as risk assessment, citizen participation, crisis communication or even the use of innovative technologies are meant to be shared between all the actors engaged in public spaces and their security as it embodies the central vector of social cohesion.

Christoph Kowalewski

How to prevent corruption and abuse of power (with a special focus on moral injury)?

Introduction

Power and corruption are relevant to everyone's life. They have in the past. They will be in the future. By now, mankind has clearly identified corruption as one of the "top 5 global worries" (IPSOS, 2023). The illusion that corruption would be only a problem of countries in the so-called „Global South" is long gone. The struggle for power in liberal democracies has become more vicious and corrupt practices on the one hand as well as presenting oneself as the anti-corruption candidate on the other, have become instrumental in getting ahead of one's political opponent. The „drain the swamp"-campaign in the US has shown how populists exploit the integrity failures of the traditional political elite in times when their strategy can be summed up as: polarize and conquer. The current US administration has recognized the danger that corruption represents by declaring it a national security risk in 2021 (White House, 2021). Now, more than ever, people who believe in democratic values must be able to answer the question: How to prevent corruption and abuse of power?

This article focuses on two subquestions taking an organizational perspective to provide practical answers:

1. Why does the abuse of power still come as no surprise today?
2. What does "moral injury" have to do with corruption and abuse of power?

While the first part presents a brief analysis of the challenges, the second part introduces a powerful concept related to trauma and mental health in an organizational prevention context to support its establishment by the compliance and integrity management community, also explaining the relationship between moral injury and whistleblowing.

"Abuse of power comes as no surprise"

The artist Jenny Holzer made the statement "Abuse of power comes as no surprise" famous when she managed to get it on a billboard in Times Square in 1982 (Artfixdaily, 2017). Four decades have passed since then. Why is the abuse of power still not surprising? Have we not learned to address the root causes, or is the problem too big?

In recent years we have seen various global movements addressing the abuse of power in its various awful manifestations, because they all have the abuse of power as their constitutive element. Black Lives Matter addresses racism, particularly police brutality; #MeToo addresses sexual abuse by men; Fridays for Future addresses the powerful fossil fuel industry that defends the status quo at the expense of future generations; the anti-corruption community addresses the „abuse of entrusted power for private gain" (Transparency International, 2020) in all its forms. Important steps have been taken: Critical mass has been achieved in each case to effectively expose the particular form of abuse of power. But have these movements sufficiently joined forces to analyze and address how power is distributed in our society, especially in the organizations in which we work and which are relevant to our lives? Such efforts could help us agree on fundamental, cross-cutting solutions to systematically prevent the abuse of power, which in turn would address each of the social ills we currently face.

It is obvious that we need to address hierarchies because they are the expression of how power is allocated in an organization. Hierarchies are not bad in themselves, neither is power. We need them to organize the societies in which we live and get things done. However, most of the hierarchical models we know were not designed by us. They are inherited. Some are very old, vertical and rigid, like the one of the Catholic Church, and some are new, horizontal and dynamic, like it can be the case of a start-up company[1].

"Abuse of power comes as no surprise" implies that we can expect abuse to manifest itself from time to time. Based on the premise that certain hierarchical structures imply a greater risk of abuse of power, it is possible

1 A start up-culture is no guarantee for fair treatment. Start-ups can have authoritarian structures built around its founder or founding group and expectations of sacrifice and self-exploitation are common byproducts.

to anticipate in which organization it will be more or less surprising, allowing a classification of organizations according to the likelihood of such abuse, based on the greatest risk situation identified. Generally speaking, the greater the power imbalance (in the absence of effective checks), the greater the likelihood of abuse. Thus, it is not surprising that abuse of power occurs in religious organizations and cults where the leader is seen as a superior being. Nor is it surprising when a landowner abuses undocumented field workers. It is no surprise when the country director of an international organization that does not have an effective decentralized monitoring infrastructure abuses power. No one should be surprised when abusive behavior occurs in a consulting firm that is designed to create rivalry among teams. Nor is abuse of power surprising in hierarchical organizations where retaliation against bona fide whistleblowers is tolerated.

We have also learned that an organization which is based on a moral mission does not automatically prevent abuse of power. The mechanisms that lead to abuse of power are essentially the same. According to the Global Corruption Barometer, corrupt practices are perceived in all sectors of society, from politics and business to civil society and the judicial system. In Germany, the former head of the „Central Office for Combating Property Crimes and Corruption in the Health Care System" in Frankfurt was recently sentenced to six years in prison for self-enrichment (Hessenschau, 2023). Currently, the head of the International Anti-Corruption Academy is suspended on suspicion of corruption (Euro ES Euro, 2023). The case is still pending, but it reinforces the message that you cannot exclude anyone. As frustrating as this realization is, ultimately it is important to look beyond illusions to identify risks and address them in a timely manner. There are no more excuses for being naive, and we should treat a mission-driven organization no differently than a for-profit one. As the saying goes: „Fool me once...". In fact, we may need to be more demanding with mission-driven organizations for the sake of their sustainability. We should not abandon trust altogether as the basis for organizational relationships. However, blind trust on the basis of good causes has led to abuses of power time and again. Unfortunately, the Russian proverb „Trust, but verify" must be a guiding principle to prevent abuse of power.

Putting "moral injury" on the compliance radar

Sometimes it is necessary to come across a term in order to know that something is, in fact, „a thing". It is similar to the experience of reading a book that you feel was written specifically for you. Examples of terms that needed to be established before the ideas behind them were widely recognized include depression, burnout, gaslighting, and mansplaining. Learning about „moral injury" can have a powerful effect on people who have been morally injured many times but have not found the right words to describe the particular sense of injustice they felt they were a part of. The great advantage of having such a term is that one can more easily identify others who have had similar experiences and realize that one is not alone. The author of this article was not aware of the term until 2021. He does not claim to be familiar with the most recent research on the subject, nor does he attempt to present the concept in sufficient detail, but he will nevertheless propose the integration of the concept in a professional context where, despite its perfect fit, it has rarely been used.

The original definition of „moral injury" was provided by psychiatrist Jonathan Shay in 1994. He considered moral injuries to be failures by leaders, resulting in „a betrayal of what's right, by someone who holds legitimate authority, in a high-stakes situation" (Shay, 2014 in: Jones, 2020). The definition and concept were developed by researchers at King's College London, among others:

> *„Moral injury is defined as the psychological distress which results from actions, or the lack of them, which violate your moral or ethical code. [...] such experiences can lead to negative thoughts about oneself or others (for example, "I am a terrible person" or "My colleagues don't care about me") as well as deep feelings of shame, guilt or disgust. These, in turn, can contribute to the development of mental health problems, including depression, PTSD and substance abuse.*
>
> *Moral injury is not unique to any particular profession. Our recent review found moral injury was experienced by a wide range of people in different professions, including journalists, police, teachers, military personnel and veterinarians from several countries. [...] moral injury can be caused by a range of experiences (for example, committing harmful acts, failing to stop the harmful acts of others or bearing witness to human suffering), with moral injury linked to poor mental health outcomes"* (Greenberg et al., 2023).

Moral injury is relevant in the context of trauma and, as noted above, can result from secondary traumatization, meaning that one does not have to be directly involved in or affected by an act of perceived injustice. Witnessing it can be enough to cause moral injury. The concept originated in the military context due to the usually more consequential acts and omissions that work in this field entails, but it is important to stress that it is applicable to all „professionals who are often exposed to challenging workplace events" (Greenberg et al., 2023). This article pursues a cross-professional perspective, promoting the consideration of moral injury in work contexts, which has been neglected. In particular, it seeks to introduce the concept to the now widely known professional field of compliance and integrity management. From a compliance and integrity perspective, a moral injury can represent a violation of compliance or integrity, which qualifies moral injury to be introduced into the scope of compliance and integrity management systems, since their raison d'être is to prevent such violations.

In any field of work, employees may uncover unethical practices within their organization, such as corruption or abuse of power. Such a situation can be described as a „challenging workplace event". Typically, employees lack the knowledge and experience to properly assess and deal with such an event. They may also doubt they can handle the situation effectively, especially if the perceived misconduct involves a superior. Moral distress and internal struggles may arise over whether to report the misconduct and take personal risks, or to remain silent to protect the job. This quote attributed to Dr. Martin Luther King Jr. provides a good explanation of this struggle: „Our lives begin to end the day we become silent about things that matter". Faced with the scenario of remaining silent and seeing it as a betrayal of one's own values, such a decision represents a struggle for integrity and one's own identity, the image one has created of oneself and the ideals one has sought to defend in one's life.

Employees who decide to come forward become what is usually called „whistleblowers"[2], a role they might have never wanted to assume. Whistleblowers tend to explain their action referring to their conscience which ultimately had not left them any choice. To put it differently: Whistleblowers are individuals who seek to prevent moral injury, thus, to

2 Alternative term: „Upstander", a term coined by Samantha Power as an antonym to „bystander" (2019).

maintain their moral integrity and avoid moral distress at the expense of the distress that the prospect of retaliation may cause. The stress that the risk of retaliation represents can be considerable, as such a „high-stakes situation" can have a significant impact on one's personal and professional life. This has often been seen in cases where whistleblowers were not only fired but have been blacklisted and have had difficulty finding another job in the industry in which they specialized.

To give an idea of the risk: During the session at the 28th German Crime Prevention Congress that is the basis for this article, the author conducted a live poll with the session's participants, asking them to anonymously agree or disagree with the statement: "I can report unethical practices without fear of retaliation". Less than half of the participants agreed with the statement (Kowalewski, 2023). More representative surveys, such as the Global Business Ethics Survey, confirm the fear of retaliation in the workplace as it still is too common an experience (Ethics & Compliance Initiative, 2023). Given this reality, it is not surprising that the phenomenon of whistleblowing is also being studied as part of the „heroism science" (Whistleblowing International Network, 2020). And as long as we need people with heroic qualities to address injustices in the workplace, it will not be possible to significantly reduce corruption and abuse of power.

Retaliation itself can have a catalytic effect. According to Garrick & Buck (2020), "retaliatory tactics can result in Workplace Traumatic Stress (WTS), which causes Moral Injury (MI) to the whistleblower and can lead to post-traumatic stress disorder (PTSD), depression, substance abuse, and even suicide". Such tactics include "gaslighting, mobbing, marginalization, shunning, devaluation, double-binding, blacklisting, counter-accusations, and emotional and physical violence" (Garrick & Buck, 2020). Shockingly, workplace violence is not as rare as one might hope[3]. Jüttner (2023) distinguishes between „pathological culture", „bureaucratic culture" and „generative culture" which indicate whether whistleblowers are scapegoated or whether constructive criticism and whistleblowing are accepted and respected.

The lack of institutional capacity to deal (constructively) with ethical dilemmas can be a reason for employees to feel particularly disappointed,

3 According to a recent survey almost every fifth employee globally experiences violence or harassment at work (International Labour Organization and Lloyd's Register Foundation 2022). Costas (2022) and Palazzo (2022) have been exploring "violence in organizations" and "normalizing violence in organizations".

even betrayed, by their employer. As employees usually tend to be loyal to their employer, this relationship is affected by moral injury and retaliation, possibly leading to "quiet quitting", a rather mild expression, or to a sense of no longer being bound by contractual obligations due to a breach of the contractual duty of care, which may lead to breach of confidentiality agreements and external whistleblowing[4].

Such consequential risks make it even more important for compliance and integrity managers to explicitly address moral injury. An effective compliance and integrity management system reduces the materialization of compliance and integrity risks, thereby minimizing events that can cause moral injury. In addition to the preventive effect, a well-developed compliance and integrity management system also has an empowering effect on employees by providing capacity building measures and integrity tools, such as a whistleblower management system or a helpdesk function, that strengthen moral agency (Ethics Unwrapped, 2022) and thus the ability to make good moral decisions without fear of being held accountable for them, or to help others find a way to resolve their ethical dilemmas appropriately. Such integrity tools, especially when first introduced, need to have low barriers to entry, because:

> *„Getting support for moral injury-related mental health difficulties can be challenging for a number of reasons. First, as moral injury can cause intense feelings of shame, guilt and disgust, those who are struggling may find it especially difficult to seek help. Those affected may also have concerns about the potential social and/or legal consequences of sharing what has happened"* (Greenberg et al., 2023).

Ideally, compliance and integrity managers do not wait for employees in known risk positions to call in, but rather act proactively and check in regularly. To be able to do this, moral injury must be part of the risk assessment exercises that identify risk positions.

Employees in leadership positions should receive special support. Because of their workload combined with a higher level of responsibility (i.e. more consequential decisions), they may be more likely to face „challenging

4 The author has been told that there have even been the first successful moral injury lawsuits in Eastern European countries but has not yet been able to verify this. If you know of any jurisdiction in the world where a claim for moral injury has been allowed to proceed, or even won, the author would appreciate such information: ckowalewski@transparency.de

workplace events". Workload is a particularly relevant aspect in this context, as ethical dilemmas represent additional work, besides moral and psychological challenges. Leaders who are overwhelmed may not deal adequately with an ethical dilemma, increasing the risk of moral injury to themselves and others. In the absence of the resources necessary to provide such help, a culture of humble leadership will result in leaders either seeking support from peers or, if possible, not being afraid to be vulnerable and consulting with subordinates to find the best possible decision.

The above-mentioned compliance and integrity initiatives should be complemented by efforts to measure their success, for instance, by using proxies that indicate the level of moral injury in an organization. To give an example, the company Glencore (2023) conducts an annual employee survey in which statements such as "My direct manager acts ethically and in compliance with policies" are put to a vote. The aggregated results are even published. Analyzing these types of proxies, especially over time, and sharing them, at least internally, can help demonstrate the reduction of events causing moral injury, identify where support is most needed and strengthen the overall culture of accountability and integrity.

Ultimately, one of the main goals of compliance and integrity management systems is to redress unhealthy power asymmetries that can lead to abuse of power and stand in the way of a more democratic and meritocratic organization that produces the best possible (moral) decisions and outcomes by allowing its members to contribute to more informed and objective decision-making processes and by increasing accountability rather than leaving all responsibility with management. A comprehensive compliance and integrity management system could also be seen as an investment in employee well-being that is money well spent (Deloitte UK, 2021) and this is a perspective that could lead the Human Resources Department to support the work of compliance and integrity colleagues. Where organizations are already working on mental health, they should ensure that those responsible seek regular interaction with compliance and integrity officers, and vice versa.

It is likely that most organizations have not adequately addressed moral injury in the past, which may have caused trauma and resulted in a lack of trust that needs to be rebuilt. Once employees recognize a genuine effort to make things right, post-traumatic growth can occur, making the organization more resilient, and providing psychological safety. These aspects are becoming increasingly important, especially to younger generations who are growing up in an era in which the issue of toxic workplaces has been the subject of intense debate. Not only because of the „war for talent," providing psychological safety in the workplace should become a goal for every organization. As long as moral injury is common, an organization will not reach its full potential.

Finally, consultants, auditors and certifiers of compliance and integrity management systems should pay attention to the issue of moral injury and raise it if it has not already been addressed in the organization to which they provide services. Rating agencies, which evaluate companies to rank those with the best working conditions, should take into account whether moral injury is explicitly prevented. And (government) institutions that define requirements for compliance and integrity management systems should include the moral injury perspective. A world in which prevention is appropriately prioritized will not only reduce moral injury, it will also reduce the need for whistleblowers, because in healthy organizations, challenging situations can be constructively addressed within one's team or hierarchy.

Conclusion

Anti-corruption expert Daniel Kaufmann once put it: "You don't fight corruption by fighting corruption" (in: Graycar, n.d.). This implies that it takes more than just focusing on the investigative and punitive aspects of anti-corruption. And it requires a broader view than just on corruption. As the article explains, in an organization with a focus on accountability and a strong speak-up culture, corruption, abuse of power and moral injury do come as a surprise, i.e., as an exception. Making the case for prevention.

From a cross-professional perspective, it has been shown how a trauma and mental health perspective is an important complement to the usual compliance, integrity and whistleblowing management discourse. And it has shown that professional and well-resourced integrity and compliance management in an organization is an indispensable asset in preventing different kinds of abuse of power in our working lives and beyond. Therefore, this article will hopefully provide compliance and integrity managers with new arguments to underline the importance and dimension of their work.

Bibliography

Artfixdaily. (2017, October, 30). Art World Circulates ‚Not Surprised' Open Letter After Artforum Scandal. https://www.artfixdaily.com/news_feed/2017/10/30/7102-art-world-circulates-not-surprised-open-letter-after-artforum-sca

Costas, J. (2022, June 17). Violence in organizations. in: Modernity Unhinged: Organized Violence in its Contexts - Academic Symposium on 1 June 2022 [Video]. YouTube. https://www.youtube.com/watch?v=aDgsqm3MH4k

Deloitte UK. (2021). Mental health and Employers: the case for investment - Pandemic and beyond. https://www2.deloitte.com/uk/en/pages/consulting/articles/mental-health-and-employers-the-case-for-investment.html

Ethics & Compliance Initiative. (2023, September 22). Global Business Ethics Survey. Ethics & Compliance Initiative. https://www.ethics.org/global-business-ethics-survey/

Ethics Unwrapped. (2022, November 5). Moral agent - ethics unwrapped. https://ethicsunwrapped.utexas.edu/glossary/moral-agent

Euro ES Euro. (2023, July 29). The head of the International Anti-Corruption Academy is suspended on suspicion of corruption. https://euro.eseuro.com/world/amp/719571

Garrick, J. & Buck, M. (2020, September 15). WHISTLEBLOWER RETALIATION CHECKLIST: A NEW INSTRUMENT FOR IDENTIFYING RETALIATORY TACTICS AND THEIR PSYCHOSOCIAL IMPACTS AFTER AN EMPLOYEE DISCLOSES WORKPLACE WRONGDOING. Published in: Crisis, Stress, and Human Resilience: An International Journal 2 (2), pp. 76–93. https://www.crisisjournal.org/article/17219-whistleblower-retaliation-checklist-a-new-instrument-for-identifying-retaliatory-tactics-and-their-psychosocial-impacts-after-an-employee-discloses-w

Glencore. (2023). Ethics and Compliance Report 2022. https://www.glencore.com/.rest/api/v1/documents/static/57a5935e-4ba6-4a26-b03f-d3fb7a0b41df/GLEN-Ethics-and-Compliance-Report-2022.pdf

Greenberg, N., Murphy, D., Stevelink, S. & Williamson, V. (2023). Moral injury: violating your ethical code can damage mental health – new research. The Conversation. https://theconversation.com/moral-injury-violating-your-ethical-code-can-damage-mental-health-new-research-115654

Hessenschau (2023, May 12). Korruptionsprozess: Früherer Frankfurter Oberstaatsanwalt zu sechs Jahren Haft verurteilt. hessenschau.de. https://www.hessenschau.de/panorama/korruptionsprozess-frueherer-frankfurter-oberstaatsanwalt-zu-sechs-jahren-haft-verurteilt-v4,urteil-prozess-oberstaatsanwalt-100.html

International Labour Organization and Lloyd's Register Foundation (2022, December 2). Experiences of violence and harassment at work: A global first survey. https://www.ilo.org/global/publications/WCMS_863095/lang--en/index.htm

IPSOS. (2023, September 25). What Worries the World - September 2023: Concern about crime reaches highest level since before the pandemic. https://www.ipsos.com/en-be/what-worries-world-september-2023-concern-about-crime-reaches-highest-level-pandemic

Jüttner, M. (2023). Die Kunst erfolgreicher Compliance, p. 391 (image of „Entscheidungs- und Fehlerkultur", see annex), on Linked-in: https://www.linkedin.com/posts/markus-j%C3%BCttner-a64b15113_entscheidung-und-fehlerkultur-in-unternehmen-ugcPost-7099750529609650177-w1Tp/

Kaufmann, D. (n. d.) in: Graycar, A. (n.d.). Criminology and Corruption, Prevention and Punishment – IACAlumni Magazine. https://magazine.iaca.int/criminology-and-corruption-prevention-and-punishment

Kowalewski, C. (2023, September 7), on LinkedIn: https://www.linkedin.com/posts/christophkowalewski_5dfv-dpt28-whistleblowingculture-activity-7105553486703943681-uB-3?utm_source=share&utm_medium=member_desktop

Palazzo, G. (2022, 17. Juni). Normalizing violence in organizations. in: Modernity Unhinged: Organized Violence in its Contexts - Academic Symposium on 1 June 2022 [Video]. YouTube. https://www.youtube.com/watch?v=aDgsqm3MH4k

Power, S. (2019). The education of an idealist: A Memoir. William Collins, pp. 127-128, 131-132.

Shay, J. (1994) Achilles in Vietnam: Combat Trauma and the Undoing of Character. Scribner, p. 183 in: Jones, E. (2020). Moral injury in a context of trauma. https://www.cambridge.org/core/journals/the-british-journal-of-psychiatry/article/moral-injury-in-a-context-of-trauma/82DE047143C9669BDFEDC81E614A8CA5

Transparency International. (2020, August 10). What is corruption? Transparency.org. https://www.transparency.org/en/what-is-corruption

Whistleblowing International Network. (2020, April 28). Call for Papers on the Heroism of Whistleblowers. https://whistleblowingnetwork.org/News-Events/News/News-Archive/Call-for-Papers-on-the-Heroism-of-Whistleblowers

White House. (2021, June 3). FACT SHEET: Establishing the fight against corruption as a core U.S. national security interest. The White House. https://www.whitehouse.gov/briefing-room/statements-releases/2021/06/03/fact-sheet-establishing-the-fight-against-corruption-as-a-core-u-s-national-security-interest/

Macarena Rau Vargas

Urban safety through women leadership

Abstract

The following article describes the application of the CPTED methodology, from a third-generation approach, in a neighborhood called Villa Andes del Sur, located in the communal limit between the Municipality of Puente Alto and La Florida, in the metropolitan region of Santiago de Chile, during 2021-2023. This villa has struggled the past three years with theft, extreme COVID and post COVID context among with social stigmatization. Third Generation CPTED (Mihinjac and Saville, 2019) incorporates relevant principles such as Sustainability, Self-realization, and Public Health Sustainability to the principles of natural surveillance, natural access control, territorial reinforcement, maintenance, and community participation from CPTED first and second generation. This article will describe how the CPTED project of Villa Andes del Sur in Puente Alto, Chile, in the context of a CPTED Masterplan increases the levels of mental health and urban safety through the women leadership.

1. Introduction

The perception of insecurity as well as the high and growing criminal opportunity in the cities of Chile, especially in its capital, Santiago, is one of the greatest concerns of its population.

This situation is in line with what is observed in Latin American cities[1] that have the highest rates of homicides among other crimes.

1 https://es.statista.com/estadisticas/1271238/america-latina-y-el-caribe-tasa-de-homicidios-intencionales-por-pais/

One of the communes with the greatest urban security challenges is Puente Alto commune in Santiago de Chile. This commune has more than 850,000 inhabitants according to the last national census and since 2000 it has been an active laboratory of CPTED applied by the CPTED Region-ICA Chapter team.

The CPTED intervention in Puente Alto has combined First Generation, Second Generation, and Third Generation CPTED.

Despite the long history of CPTED interventions in Puente Alto, in Chile has increased the criminal opportunity, which has impacted the criminogenic context of Puente Alto also. The year 2019 saw a social insurrection in Chile, that caused the Chilean President of that time, Sebastián Piñera, to almost resign his post in the face of strong demonstrations and acts of terrorism like bombs, fire, explosions in subway stations among others in the country.

A constituent process was agreed to make changes to the Constitution, which in 2023 will delivered the new draft to be approved or not by the citizens in a plebiscite.

On the other hand, the communities of Chile, including Puente Alto, faced, like the world population, a COVID and post COVID pandemic context, which affected health, safe, economic, and emotional stability of the inhabitants.

In this context and as an intervention to support vulnerable groups, Mayor Germán Codina from Puente Alto, asked CPTED Region-ICA Chapter team in July 2021, led by Dr. Macarena Rau, to support, with a complete cycle of the CPTED Project, a population that is on the edge between Puente Alto and Florida called Villa Andes del Sur. The great and main characteristic of this community is that it is composed mostly of older women.

From July 2021 to August 2023 the CPTED process in Andes del Sur has been very rich in experiences and research.

The community of older adults has not only managed to reorganize and heal itself in an emotional situation of catastrophe and grief but has also been able to provide support and assistance to other communities in Puente Alto applying CPTED strategies.

2. Literature review

In the process of preparing and implementing the CPTED Master Plan for the Villa Andes del Sur in Puente Alto, from July 2021 to August 2023, numerous bibliographical sources have been reviewed. From the CPTED perspective the reviewed literature was numerous as follows:

The first one was the Manual de Espacios Urbanos Seguros[2] (Rau, Macarena et al. 2003) wrote many years ago but still available in the Ministry of Housing webpage, to learn about first-generation CPTED with its principles of Natural Surveillance, Natural Access Control, Territorial Reinforcement and Maintenance. This publication was the first in Chile to describe the CPTED methodology, but it also provides concrete examples of good and bad practices of the application of CPTED in social housing environments, such as the case of Villa Andes del Sur. Unfortunately, this Manual doesn't include formally CPTED second generation, so it's limited in its view. A second publication that was a great contribution to the elaboration of the CPTED diagnosis and Master Plan in Villa Andes del Sur was the INVI[3] article of the year 2008 (Rau, Macarena. Castillo, Paulina. 2008) in which the relevance of the design of spaces was studied considering residential and housing typologies with wide visual fields to increase natural surveillance.

A third relevant publication was the article about Fear Perception in Residential Settings[4] (Macarena Rau V, Ivan Cartes, Francisco Gatica & Tim Pascoe.2018). This article not only describes the relevance of Second-Generation CPTED. "The principle of community participation" is integral to competent CPTED practice and Second Generation CPTED is based on that but also describes, breaks down and analyze es the perception of insecurity of crime invulnerable communities in Latin America through self-administered surveys.

2 Rau, Macarena et al.2003. Manual de Espacios Urbanos Seguros. Santiago, Chile, www.cpted.cl/publicaciones

3 Macarena Rau, Paulina Castillo. 2008. REVISTA INVI_64.indd 170 21/11/2008 10:07:17 ARTÍCULO: Prevención de la violencia y el delito mediante el diseño ambiental en Latinoamérica N° 64 // Volumen N° 23: 169-189 171

4 Macarena Rau V, Ivan Cartes, Francisco Gatica & Tim Pascoe (2018) Impact Evaluation of Situational Prevention Strategies and CPTED (Crime Prevention through Environmental Design) in Vulnerable Neighborhoods in Latin America, Journal of Applied Security Research, 13:4, 437-454, DOI: 10.1080/19361610.2018.1498254

Another article that was very useful in the context of a local municipal CPTED intervention was "City & Security communities and citizens' rights in the co-production of security"[5] (Van Den Shuren, Franz et al. 2020) From this article the main idea of local governance and co-production of security was considered in the Villa Andes del Sur CPTED Masterplan.

Form a participatory diagnosis process the CPTED article "Tercera Generación: Diagnóstico de Percepción Infantil la Nube de los Sueños" (Rau Vargas, M. 2021) was useful to understand one aspect of the Cloud of Dreams methodology, in particular the role of the dreaming process in children and adults especially where the mental health of community members has been impacted, as occurred during COVID with Villa Andes del Sur.

Finally, the article "Third-Generation Crime Prevention Through Environmental Design (CPTED)" (Mihinjac and Saville, 2019) was studied. In this article, the authors consider that from its origins C. Ray Jeffery had a holistic and comprehensive vision of CPTED and that this third generation incorporates the search for habitability through new principles such as economic, social, environmental and public health sustainability, aspects that are critically important in the COVID context of mental health.

3. Methodology

In Villa Andes del Sur, the aim was to implement a complete cycle of the CPTED Project; this is a four phases process with diagnostic, design, implementation, and evaluation in a participatory context as suggested by ISO CPTED standard 22341.

In July 2021, the CPTED diagnosis began in Villa Andes del Sur with the municipal team of the Public Security Directorate led by Mrs. Olga González del Riego and Dr. Macarena Rau Vargas, ICA President.

To carry out the diagnosis, several diagnostic instruments were applied to obtain both primary and secondary information. Regarding secondary information, it was collected from the police station Commissariat 38 Pu-

5 Van Den Shuren, Franz et al. City & Security Communities and citizens' rights in the co-production of security, LAP LAMBERT Academic Publishing (2020-06-02), SBN-13: 978-620-0-55087-3, ISBN-10:6200550875, EAN: 9786200550873

ente Alto, to verify the criminal profile of the neighborhood. Instruments were applied to collect primary information directly from the community, such as Security Exploratory March, that is a Safety Audit process done with the community walking around the neighborhood, ESU (Urban Security Survey), CPTED Direct Observation, among others described below.

3. 1 Criminal context of Villa Andes del Sur

Location

Villa Andes del Sur is in the northern sector of Puente Alto, in Santiago-Chile bordering La Florida, to the west with Av. Concha y Toro, with an abundant flow of private vehicles and public transport. Towards the south-west of such avenue is the Elisa Correa Metro station, supermarkets, minor stores, a service center, etc. To the east it borders with other stages of Villa Andes del Sur.

Sociodemographic characterization

According to data from the 2017 Census, it registers a total population of 3,104 people (53% women and 47% men), 987 households, 670 dwellings[6]. At the educational level, 72% of the population have secondary or higher education (24% technical / 18% university), and finally the composition by age ranges without distinguishing sex is 35% elderly (60 or older), 27% between 30 to 59 years old and 38% between 0 to 29 years old.

Equipment

The Villa is mainly residential, with the presence of minor businesses inside, schools on its outer edges, it has 7 green areas (small to medium size), these with games/exercise machines inside and 2 multi-courts (1 alone and 1 integrated to the previous equipment).

3. 2 Robbery with violence in Villa Andes del Sur (2020)

Among the different crimes registered in the Villa Andes del Sur sector (in all its stages), robbery with violence or intimidation registers a greater number of police cases (complaints + arrests) for 2020, concentrating

6 INE. Censo Población Chilena. 2017.

in particular (map) from Los Toros Street to the north. In this research, the complaints and arrest records were combined because of the lack of training of the police local team. The total robbery cases, 95% occurred on public roads and the remaining % in private homes, mainly during the afternoon/night and early morning, 22% between 4:00 p.m. and 7:59 p.m., 34% between 8:00 p.m. and 11:00 p.m. :59 hours, 17% in range 04:00 - 07:59 hours. Then, specifically for Andes del Sur, the registered cases are concentrated around the axis of Nemesio Vicuña, La Portada, Bahía Inglesa and Cochoa streets.

Although the composition for this sector is varied, the above could indirectly generate some problems. The green area contains exercise machines, accompanied by a multi-court, as well as commercial premises of various kinds and even a liquor store.

The configuration of the sector could allow hiding places for criminals, facilitating their escape, etc., hindering their natural surveillance.

3. 3 Urban Layout

Villa Andes del Sur is spatially organized around Salvador San Fuentes Street through closed passages with a few small squares. It has a neighbourhood headquarters and a court that, due to the COVID pandemic during 2020, remained closed and only began to function in July 2021 when the CPTED strategy began.

The few squares were filled with vandalism and graffiti during the pandemic period, as well as garbage, which greatly increased the perception of insecurity among older adults who remained locked up in their homes until July 2021.

An Exploratory Security March was carried out with residents of the sector day and night to assess their environmental perception of the environment and interesting results were obtained.

Picture 1. Exploratory Security March in Villa Andes del Sur.

Another diagnostic instrument applied was the Cloud of Dreams with children and elderly.

Picture 2. Confined places with grafitti where one can be hidden from the sight of others

Picture 3. Elderly Cloud of Dream workshop

Repetition of elements

Seven analysis filters were applied to the sample of drawings and the repetition of elements in the total sample was measured, highlighting the need for contact with nature and games.

Picture 4. Lula's dream was a beautiful tree with flowers and nice landscaping.

4. The Problem in Villa Andes del Sur

After analyzing all the evidence and information collected in the CPTED diagnosis, the problem to work on is crime: robbery, incivilities (litter, graffiti etc.), lack of urban management/maintenance (cleaning and public lighting) and feelings of insecurity.

For this strategy to be relevant to Third Generation CPTED, it considers the central principles of 3rd Gen:

A. Public Health Sustainability: the mental health of the old people after COVID context will be activated with activities to increase art in public space, identity, and sense of belonging.

B. Environmental Sustainability: different activities of gardening will teached to the old people in Andes del Sur so they can grow their own vegetables and fruits.

C. Economic Sustainability: Different workshops of art crafts willl be teached like mosaics so they can earn money selling this art craft.

D. Social Sustainability: this aspect is key for the CPTED Plan and integrates activities to increase social cohesion among old people and younger members of the community.

5. The CPTED Masterplan for Villa Andes del Sur

It is proposed to the community to develop a CPTED Master Plan after de diagnosis that aims to accomplish the following goals:

- To reduce criminal spatial vulnerability by maintenance and order of public space,
- To increase the levels of habitability and mental health of the community, and
- To increase the levels of social cohesion, especially in the group of older adults.

This Master Plan will have several components, the work of trust being the construction of a community mosaic that tells the founding history of the neighborhood considering the memory of the grandparents. The expected outcome is to increase social cohesion among elderlies and from them to their families to increase levels of comfort, wellbeing, trust. For this, together with the Department of Culture and Public Safety of the Municipality, training workshops are started for grandmothers in the Mosaic technique for beginners.

In the first meetings there were not many grandmothers since the trust for the activity had not yet been created. Eventually, through three months of persistence, conditions improved with more enjoyable activities and relaxation in addition to a mosaic led by the President of the Neighborhood Council, Mrs. Carolina Cancino. She and the group of elderly's supporting her were very resilient and through some local wisdom was able to guide her community and support the CPTED Master Plan since its inception.

Mrs. Carolina Cancino and other Elder in Villa Andes de Sur believes that the collective work of the other grandmothers in the community should be based on an idea of exchange and mutual support. Many of the grandmothers sell handicrafts and by working in the community mosaic they can display their handicrafts at a neighborhood venue. Ultimately, it is a win-win community entrepreneurship model.

In this sense the value exchange for collective well-being done by elder in Villa Andes del Sur connects with third generation CPTED.

Picture 5. Timeline of Villa Andes del Sur in mosaics.

Another aspect of Mrs. Carolina Cancino's leadership together with all the elderly's that support her leadership is to honor the memory workshop where the grandmothers remembered important and historical moments in their process of populating Villa Andes del Sur.

6. Discussion and conclusion

Based on the results of the CPTED participatory diagnosis as a first step in the process of implementing the Master Plan in the case study, a complete and positive socio environmental change has been done with Andes del Sur community lead by Carolina Cancino, leader of the Neighborhood association.

As the CPTED process of participatory community mosaics progressed, the community's level of joy and self-realization increased, and they stopped requesting support and installation of video surveillance cameras. Their environmental needs regarding urban security changed.

In the success and recovery of mental health by the grandparents in the case study, the strong leadership of Mrs. Carolina Cancino supported by many old people in the Villa has been a major success factor.

References

Rau, Macarena et al.2003. Manual de Espacios Urbanos Seguros. Santiago, Chile.

Macarena Rau, Paulina Castillo. 2008. REVISTA INVI_64.indd 170 21/11/2008 10:07:17

ARTÍCULO: Prevención de la violencia y el delito mediante el diseño ambiental en Latinoamérica N° 64 / / Volumen N° 23: 169-189 171

Macarena Rau V, Ivan Cartes, Francisco Gatica & Tim Pascoe (2018) Impact Evaluation of Situational Prevention Strategies and CPTED (Crime Prevention through Environmental Design) in Vulnerable Neighborhoods in Latin America, Journal of Applied Security Research, 13:4, 437-454, DOI: 10.1080/19361610.2018.1498254

Van Den Shuren, Franz et al. City & Security Communities and citizens' rights in the co-production of security, LAP LAMBERT Academic Publishing (2020-06-02), SBN-13: 978-620-0-55087-3, ISBN-10:6200550875, EAN: 9786200550873

Mihinjac, Mateja, and Gregory Saville. 2019. "Third-Generation Crime Prevention Through Environmental Design (CPTED)" Social Sciences 8, no. 6: 182. https://doi.org/10.3390/socsci8060182

Macarena Rau, Francisco Gatica, Iván Cartes, Thimothy Pascoe, Víctor Carrasco, Perception of Criminal Insecurity in Vulnerable Districts in Latin America, Urban and Regional Planning. Volume 4, Issue 4, December 2019, pp. 121-135. doi: 10.11648/j.urp.20190404.11

Jacobs, J. (1962). Death and life of Great American Cities, New York: Vintage Books.

Macarena Rau, CPTED de Tercera Generación, Diagnóstico de Percepción Infantil la "Nube de los Sueños", Revista Constructos Criminológico, UANL, México, 2019.

Obando, Obando, Julio César, La Minga: un instrumento vivo para el Desarrollo comunitario, Revista de Sociolgía ISSN 1900-5547, Universidad de Nariño, 2018.

Pozo Menares, Canio Llanquinao, M., & Neculfilu, C. (2014). Wenumapu : astronomía y cosmología mapuche (1a ed.). Ocho Libros Editores.

ICA Guidebook. CPTED in Schools a comprehensive approach. ICA School Committee, 2022.

Garza, Tonatiuh, Naciendo a la vida: Mezcalito y el Temazcal, (Kindle Edition) Published August 17th, 2017, Kindle Edition, 166 pages

Joost N. Kok, Egbert J. W. Boers, Walter A. Kosters, Peter van der Putten and Mannes Poel ,Artificial Intelligence: Definition, Trends, Techniques and Cases -, 2012.

John Rook

The Decriminalization of Poverty

It was a pleasure to speak at the "Crisis and Prevention" German Prevention Congress in Mannheim Germany in June 2023. My presentation, entitled "Criminalization of Poverty" looked at a brief history of the issue and some possible solutions. Thank you to the conference organizers for allowing me the opportunity to speak, and to the participants who showed enthusiasm for the presentation and shared some interesting ideas from their own contexts. Thank you to my hosts, Petra Guder and Prof. Dr. Bernd-Rüdeger Sonnen, who so graciously took care of my every need while in Germany.

In this chapter we will look at several solutions to the Criminalization of Poverty such as the Prolific Offender Engagement Team (POET) Program, The Calgary Drug Court, the Alberta Home Visitation Network Association (AHVNA, and Simon House Recovery Centre where I currently work. I begin by mentioning Encampments, which I did not discuss in my previous work nor at the conference, but which has become a major issue in many North American cities.

Brief History of the Problem

People who are in poverty have a greater chance of being arrested than people who are not in poverty.[1] There is a long history of this fact in both Europe and North America. The pre-incarceration of people in USA prisons shows that the incomes of the incarcerated are less than half of those in the general population.[2] While many countries have tried to

---

1 John Rook and Samantha Sexsmith, "The Criminalization of Poverty," in John A. Winterdyk (ed), Crime Prevention: International Perspectives, Issues and Trends, CRC Press, 2017, 317-344.

2 Rook, 2017, Table 12.1, page 326.

find solutions to this problem, the problem continues to exist. In Canada, while 10% live in poverty, in 2010, 62% of those in federal prison were unemployed at the time of their arrest.[3] While our previous work focused mainly on the problem of Poverty and Crime, in this chapter we will consider several solutions that are in play in my home city of Calgary, Alberta, Canada.

In many North American cities, even with the practice of Housing First in place, many homeless encampments have sprung up. People who live in these encampments have little or no money, are usually unemployed, have no formal housing, are either fearful of shelters (hostels in some countries) or the shelters are full. Mental health concerns and drug use are often prevalent. You can read many articles on the internet about these "illegal encampments" and how cities are dismantling them often without a plan for those who are displaced. Calgary has the JET Team (Joint Encampment Team) and the PAL Team (Partner Agency Liaison Team) who work with the occupants if it is an active site, to assist them with a move to an appropriate social agency for support. The occupants are usually given up to 72 hours to vacate the site unless there is no housing alternative. The site is then cleaned up which usually means that all personal items which the occupant couldn't take with them, are destroyed.[4] The lack of housing everywhere and NIMBY (Not in My Back Yard) is rampant.

A major concern with this is that how we deal with encampments is like how we traditionally have dealt with other social ills, namely that our solutions deal with the "what" of the issue, not the "why" of the issue. We observe the "what" but need to understand the "why." When we understand the why, we will more likely treat people with respect and find solutions. The why of encampments is poverty. A lack of income is solvable. A lack of housing is solvable. A lack of safety is solvable.

To ensure that we understand poverty in the context of the discussion, I will share a definition which my students at the Canadian Poverty Institute developed as it is a good working definition. The students believed

3 Chelsey Legge, "The Poverty-Crime Connection: A Case for reducing the Government Filing Fee for Pardons/Record Suspensions," from www.pardonapplications.ca (accessed December 25, 2023)

4 "Encampments: Calgary's approach to illegal encampments" from www.calgary.ca (accessed December 25, 2023)

correctly that poverty is multi-faceted.[5] My personal growing up story is one of economic poverty, but we were relationally rich with a close-knit family, a wonderful neighbourhood community, and a strong church connection. It wasn't until I went to university that I realized that we were economically poor. The definition the students developed was this: "A person is in poverty when their human dignity has been compromised by the social, political and/or religious structures of this society. This results in a state of existence where their resources and assets deny them opportunity to live in good health and happiness."[6]

I had a wonderful friend who died a few years ago who taught me so much about poverty, homelessness, and addiction. His name was John B and we met in the Salvation Army's Centre of Hope in Calgary. It is a large homeless shelter where John was a client when I was the Chief Executive. John told me that there were three phases to his life. In Phase One, he became a successful business owner, got married, had children, and eventually had grandchildren. It wasn't until Phase Three that he realized that in Phase One, he had blocked all his early childhood trauma. By blocking it, he was able to live a normal life. He felt successful and seemed happy.

In Phase Two, John went through a divorce, and he started to have flashbacks to his trauma days. Soon they were overwhelming him, and he didn't know what to do. He was at a friend's house one day who was using cocaine. His friend offered him some and instantly he was hooked. It took away all his pain, and for a while he felt good. For him, the drug was a huge coping mechanism that brought him instant relief from the thoughts in his head. Soon he was not only divorced, but he was disowned by his children, lost his business, and ended up sell drugs to feed his new habit. This went on for thirteen years and when I met him, John was living in our homeless shelter. We had over 300 beds and a 37 bed addictions floor which John applied for and was accepted. About that time, his grandson died in a car chase while fleeing from a drug dealer who was trying to collect from him. That was devastating for John as he had to bury his grandson. At the funeral he was able to reconnect with some family and that began John's Phase Three. In this phase, John dealt with his trauma with a counsellor, got clean and stayed clean. He also was

5 In the class they considered economic, education, health, spiritual/cultural, political, societal as well as situational, relative, absolute, and generational.

6 The Shock Poverty Class, Ambrose University, 2011

able to get a small apartment and now that he was over 65 years old, he received the Canada Pension Plan which was enough to live on if he was careful.

John used his time well in Phase Three. Along with some professors from the University of Calgary and me, we started The Downtown Community Initiative, a program that university students, staff from the homeless shelter, and clients from the shelter were in class together. John loved that program, told his story to the students, and took the university students on "homeless walks" to show them how people who were homeless lived and survived on the streets. He knew all the homeless people who lived rough on the streets, and that was a wonderful learning for me and the students.

There is a Phase Four to his life story as he went into the hospital with some major issues that were a result of his drug use. My wife and I visited him regularly in the hospital and one day he asked my wife to get him a coffee. When she returned with it, he sat up in the bed and savoured a few sips. We told him we were leaving as we had to pick up our son from school and he said, "I love you guys." Those were the last words we heard him say as he died the next day.

The connection to the criminalization of poverty for John was in his Phase Two. He was picked up for minor crimes and spent time in jail. He was known to many of the police and not one ever offered him help or a solution. They only arrested him. I won't go into it here, but we know that the cost of his crime which includes police, ambulance, court, and hospital costs were astronomical. There is much evidence that shows us the extreme savings if we can direct those dollars to living supports instead of incarceration.

As I mentioned earlier, the problem of poverty and criminality is not new. In the 1800s in both the United Kingdom and the United States of America, people were banished to poor houses.[7] This was thought to be a deterrent to crime and begging but the evidence shows that it did not work. People died in these houses at an alarming rate. Another solution that followed poor houses where homeless shelters and hostels. These keep people alive, but often that is all they do. In one shelter where I was the Chief Executive, I made the decision to make a few changes. First, I

7 Rook, 2017, p. 319.

changed the title of the front-line staff from Shelter Workers to Exit Strategists. Staff then knew that their job was not to simply give people a meal and a bed, but it was to help them exit positively. Along with this change, we put supports in place like a housing worker, employment coaches and a chaplain. These supports, and the simple change of title, changed the statistical outputs and outcomes significantly.[8]

There are many factors which exacerbate the problem. In Calgary, an average 1-bedroom apartment, if it were available, would cost you about $1,775 CDN. In the Province of Alberta where Calgary is located, someone who is on social assistance will receive $790 to $824 for those "expected to work" and $919 to $959 for those with "barriers to full employment." For AISH (Assured Income for the Severely Handicapped) recipients, they receive $1,863. If someone on AISH receives the full benefit and has a 1-bedroom apartment, they would have $88.00 remaining for food, transportation, et cetera for the month. This person would be allowed to earn up to an additional $1,072-$2,009 per month. That money is taxed at 50%. Anything over $2,009 per month is completely clawed back by the government which in effect, is a 100% tax on that income! I know of no one, except those in poverty, who are taxed 100%.

With the homeless crisis and encampments springing up in Alberta, the current government is spending on policing in a move to manage the homeless/crime problem. The Edmonton police budget was just increased from $355,000,000 to $452,000,000. Recently 245 more Sheriffs were added to the Alberta budget at a cost of $27,000,000 per year. Imagine if this money had been used for housing instead of additional policing.[9]

The other thing we see in Alberta and beyond is legislation that fines homeless people who have no income. Then there is a warrant issued, followed by an arrest, which is followed by jail time. With all the costs associated with a rather minor infraction, this makes absolutely no sense. Once again, it is spending good money after bad and solves nothing.

A perfect example of police dealing with the "what" and not understanding the "why" happens when someone is arrested for urinating in public.

8 John Rook, "A New Model of Care," in James Hughes (ed), Beyond Shelter: Solutions to Homelessness in Canada From The Front Lines. Toronto: James Lorimer & Company Ltd., 2018, pp. 161-176.

9 "Police being used as 'scapegoat' in debate over Edmonton 7% tax increase" Retrieved from www.edmonton.ctvnews.ca December 26, 2023.

If there are no toilets available, sometimes people have no option. I see this as related to the question of hostile architecture. This is an intentional strategy which is designed to restrict behaviour. We see it with spikes on grates where you cannot sleep to get warm, thorny plants placed against buildings so you can't rest there, and signs that say "You can't pee for free! Restrooms are for customers only!" and "No public Restrooms." When a city hasn't accommodated for a natural bodily function and arrests poor people because of it, that is criminalization of people in poverty.

Above, I noted that 62% of those in Canadian prisons were unemployed before incarceration. Canadian prisoners also report a low educational achievement rate, around 54% have less than a Grade 10 education. And to compound the problem, individuals with criminal records face significant discrimination when seeking employment upon release.[10] It is worth noting that where I currently work, a large percentage of our staff have moved through the courts, prison, addiction programs into recovery and are now employed with us. This is a destigmatizing strategy and treats people with dignity and respect.

Many of my staff who went through the negative side of our society can speak of childhood trauma. Most people who are imprisoned in Canada report having experienced adverse childhood events such as witnessing family violence, having one and sometimes two parents absent, involvement with the child welfare system and more than 50% have experienced physical, sexual, and emotional abuse.[11] While mental health concerns in the general population (for any disorder) is approximately 43%, in the Edmonton Alberta incarcerated population, the prevalence is 91.7%. In the provinces of Ontario and British Columbia, 80% in youth detention meet the criteria for at least one mental health disorder (DSM V) compared to 30.6% of the general population. It is also no surprise that most inmates surveyed at intake report having recently used drugs or alcohol prior to admission to custody.

Communicable and sexually transmitted diseases are also prevalent. Tuberculosis is common in the federal inmate population at 22.4% compared to 4.6% in the general population. There are high levels of

10 "Office of the Correctional Investigator Annual Report 2019-2020" Ministry of Public Safety and Emergency Preparedness, Government of Canada 2020. Retrieved from https://www.oci-bec.gc.ca/cnt/rpt/annrpt/annrpt20192020-eng.aspx

11 F. Kouyoumdjian, "Health Status of Prisoners in Canada," Canadian Family Physician 62(3), 2016.

blood borne infections such as hepatitis C and HIV. Levels of chlamydia and gonorrhea are much higher than the general population. Another factor is that more than 50% of men who are incarcerated were found to have evidence of a traumatic brain injury.

With such chaos in their lives, it makes sense that to avoid the mental pain, a person would mask it with drugs.[12] With no money, no housing, and no hope, petty crimes become a survival strategy. To eat, people resort to break and enter in homes and cars, selling drugs to pay for their own habit, and survival sex. Teens, females, and Indigenous women have very high rates of survival sex in the homeless population.[13]

In Canada, Indigenous people are admitted to prisons at an alarming rate, and it is mostly for survival crimes. In 2020/2021, Indigenous adults accounted for approximately one third of all adult admissions to prisons, 31% provincial and 33% federal but the total Indigenous population in Canada is only 5%. In the same year, 50% of all youth incarcerations were Indigenous while Indigenous youth represent only 8% of the total Canadian youth population.

Where I work at Simon House Recovery Centre, we have diligently worked to provide quality care for our Indigenous clients. In 2022 we provided 1,860 individual counselling sessions, 1285 therapy groups, we held 298 smudges not including our morning meditation and smudge which is held daily. Our Indigenous active treatment program completion rate in 54.9%.[14]

Solutions

With this brief overview of some of the concerns faced in the work of crime and poverty, we turn to some solutions that are making an impact in Calgary. First, I will describe Simon House Recovery Centre.[15] At Simon

12 Gabor Matte, In the Realm of Hungry Ghosts: Close Encounters with Addiction. Vintage Canada, 2008.

13 "Adult and Youth Correctional Statistics, 2020/2021" Statistics Canada. Retrieved from https://www.statcan.gc.ca/n1/en/daily-quotidien/220420/dq220420c-eng.pdf?st=MlYnuWtg

14 Taken from Simon House Recovery Centre FYldb database.

15 For a more full understanding of the work of Simon House, visit our website at www.simonhouse.com where you can see descriptions of the services provided, stories of impact, a copy of our Annual Reports, and you can sign up for our monthly Newsletter.

House we say the opposite of addiction is not sobriety, it is connection. With that in mind, throughout treatment, and especially near the end of the program, we begin talking about life beyond Simon House. That is where real recovery happens. We work on housing options, employment, reconnection to family, building a strong alumni, and finding a sponsor who can guide you to solutions when you hit a problem area in your life. The Indigenous program includes smudging and sweats. As I write this, two van loads of indigenous clients are on their way to the Tsuut'ina reserve to take part in a sweat.

We believe that you must understand people and their personal, cultural and spiritual needs before you can offer a healing journey to recovery. With that in mind, we have built Stonewall Recovery[16] which is Canada's first 2SLGBTQ+ addiction recovery centre. The brainchild of Steve Archambault and Brittany Sawyer, we recognized that people in the queer community were often bullied out of traditional programs and so Stonewall was created to provide a safe place for treatment. As you can imagine, the trauma is sometimes different, but our goals are the same.

Simon House Recovery Centre in Calgary, Alberta Canada, is a small step in people's lives to assist them to move from a life of trauma and scarcity to a life of abundance. Our treatment program is built on three phases, BE, BELONG, BECOME. In the BE phase of treatment, clients (we call them Residents because it is their home for 12 weeks) begin with an Orientation week. These new residents are introduced to the program, meet all the staff, learn the rules, and settle into their room and all of the expectations of the full program. In week two, they begin the BE phase of the program where they take a deep look at themselves with a counsellor and group therapy. The middle section of the program is BELONGING where residents work on connections to their higher power, their community, their family, and their future support system. Finally, in the BECOME phase, the goal is to support the resident to find successful housing, employment, and supports. We talk about what they need in their Recovery Tool Kit to ensure that they remain sober and safe. At our Commencement Ceremony which follows the program completion, each resident is given a tool kit, they are welcomed into the alumni, and the room is full of family and support people to assist them on their way. After one year of recovery, if they have remained sober, we put their

16 https://www.stonewallrecovery.ca

name on a plaque, and it is added to our wall. The wall is full of hundreds of success stories from our 10,000+ who have passed through our doors since 1984![17]

Calgary Drug Treatment Court

Many of our clients come to us through the CDTC (Calgary Drug Treatment Court). What follows is a brief description of its operation. It has a wonderful VISION: Safe communities free from the impact of drug related crime. This is a perfect way to support people who are doing criminal activities by offering them programs like Simon House. The CDTC has three OBJECTIVES:

- To reduce recidivism
- To lower costs
- To build safe communities

To enter their program, you are screened by a member of the Calgary Police Services and a Crown Prosecutor. You will be accepted if your crimes were non-violent, related to drug trafficking and property related offences. Everyone in their program is assigned a Case Worker. They provide a pre-sentence justice alternative for individuals facing charges driven by drug addiction. They integrate justice, health and treatment services with the goal of empowering individuals to restore their lives and become productive members of their community.[18] There are five stages to their program:

Stage 1: Twelve Week intensive drug treatment. In this stage, many come to Simon House.

Stage 2: The Case Manager develops an individualized treatment plan designed to increase their Recovery Capital. The basis of the work with their Case Manager is on Criminal Addictive Thinking.

Stage 3: Is a practice stage to incorporate skills learned into daily living.

Stage 4: Community Transition relocates the participant into the community.

17 Since 2019, 1103 men have gone through the Simon House Recovery Centre. 8.4% or 93 self-reported prison time. Of the 93 individuals, 37.6% completed the program.

18 https://calgarydrugtreatmentcourt.org/about-us/

Stage 5: Graduation where they return to the court for final sentencing which usually results in a non-custodial sentence.

The OUTCOMES of the Drug Treatment Court program are excellent. Since 2007, 48% have completed the program. 76% of those have received no new convictions since graduation.[19] 70% fewer charges have been laid since graduation, and 67% have fewer or no contacts with the police. In a four-year study, the COST SAVINGS are outstanding:

- $76,000,000 in the cost of stolen goods,
- $7,000,000 in incarceration costs,
- Over $300,000 saved in police responses for the 45 graduates in the study,
- Over $400,000 saved in the cost of delivering warrants to the 45 graduates.

This all works in harmony with the provincial model of a Recovery Oriented System of Care.[20]

Prolific Offender Engagement Team

Another important program that moves the needle to decriminalize poverty and those who do crime to survive is the POET (Prolific Offender Engagement Team) program.[21] This is a policing program that attempts to work on the "why" and not just the "what" of criminal behaviour. Most of Calgary's property crime is committed by a small group of offenders who are "prolific" and are well known to the police. These offenders are generally non-violent, and their crimes are for survival. Break and enter, car theft, robberies, and illegal drug sales are committed to feed their drug habit. The police officers who work on the POET team work on a positive release plan for the offender when they are released from jail. One of their main purposes is to end the catch and release system. The POET program works closely with the drug court, family members, and agencies like Simon House to assist the offender to leave their lifestyle of crime behind.

19 https://calgarydrugtreatmentcourt.org/addressing-the-cycle-of-crime-and-addiction/
20 www.calgarydrugtreatmentcourt.org/recovery-oriented-systems-of-care-ab/
21 See the Calgary Herald article, July 14, 2017 at www.calgaryherald.com

If the offender goes into an addiction program, there is strict reporting and follow up. Any breaches are dealt with swiftly. Because the POET team works closely with the Crown Prosecutor's Office and Probation, the overall success rate is excellent.

At Simon House, our current alumni President is a former POET participant. Richie C came to Simon House in September 2021, reluctant to attend an addiction recovery program. He had two options: attend the program or go to prison. It took Richie several months to figure out that he really needed to change. After completing the program, his counsellor recommended that he join the Simon House AfterCARE program[22] which he did. As I write this, Richie is celebrating 31 months in recovery and was just elected President of the Simon House Alumni Association! He is employed fulltime and not only does he have a strong alumni family, he also has his bio family back in his life. Richie says it is shocking for him to think about where he was before the program which led to his recovery! We have pictures of him in recovery with his arms around his arresting officers. When Richie is asked why this worked for him, he says what so many in the program say, "Someone believed in me. People showed me that I wasn't a useless human being, that I was worth supporting. Through their program of compassion and hope, they rehumanize people, that is what POET and Simon House did for me."[23] He continued that it was either prison or treatment and now that he is in recovery, he feels loved and he gets to love. With his attitude of gratitude, he is either winning or learning. He says, "No more loser mentality!"[24]

What police have learned from these programs is that just because you have the right to arrest which leads to conviction and incarceration, it does not mean that it's always the right thing to do. Again, by thinking about the "why" of the behaviour and not just the "what" of the behaviour, that will help determine our decisions and actions as we all work to create vibrant citizens and safe communities.

22 See the website at www.simonhouse.com

23 Conversation September 27, 2023

24 See the story of another staff member of Simon House with a long history of trauma, abuse and contact with the police, courts and prison system in Kerry Gladue, Second Chances: The Kerry Gladue Story. Brave Communications, 2018.

Universal Basic Income[25]

As mentioned earlier, lack of income produces poverty and often causes a person to do crime to survive. Many proponents of a Guaranteed Livable Annual Income believe that providing a basic income to people would significantly reduce the need for survival crime which would take the strain off the very costly police, court, and prison systems.[26] I believe that a Basic Income could be a solution to the criminalization of poverty, especially when someone is released from prison. Because it is difficult to find employment with a criminal record, a Basic Income could ensure that one does not have to resort to further criminal activity to survive.[27] The authors rightly claim that "A basic income has the potential to break these cycles of oppression by offering individuals and communities the means for greater choice and opportunity."[28] For someone leaving prison, a basic income could level the playing field and offer a sense of income stability.[29] Their conclusion supports the thesis of this chapter: "… a basic income could decriminalize poverty, support the migration of formerly incarcerated individuals, and eliminate crime as a necessary means of survival."[30]

25 See the website https://basicincomecanada.org for a discussion of the potential impact of implementing a Basic Income in Canada. Both the Parliament (C-233) and the Senate (S-223) have Basic Incomes bills before them. If passed, this would provide every Canadian with a Basic Income. Currently in Canada all persons over the age of 65 qualify for an Old Age Security pension which is a form of Basic Income. Canada also has a CCB (Canada Child Benefit) which provides a monthly tax-free amount to eligible families to assist with the cost of raising children under the age of eighteen. This is also a form of Basic Income.

26 In the 1970's in Canada, there was a basic income pilot that ran for four years. It was called MINcome and was run in Dalphin, Manitoba. One of the significant outcomes was that a guaranteed livable income was associated with a decline in crime. The provision of a basic income reduced the crime rate by 1,400 per 100,000 people. Most of the impact was a reduction in property crimes.

27 Hannah Owczar, Shelby Kendra Downe and Cloe Halpenny, "Basic Income: The Case for Criminal Justice," retrieved from www.static1.squarespace.com December 26, 2023

28 Ibid., p.2

29 Ibid., p.2

30 Ibid., p.3

Alberta Home Visitation Network Association[31]

Finally, let me end with a story. A few years ago, I was Director of Child & Family Services for the Salvation Army in Calgary, and we started a Healthy Families program based on the model of AHVNA (Alberta Home Visitation Network Association). We trained and were supported by Betsy Dew, who had worked for Healthy Families America and was the Founder and Executive Director of Great Kids Inc. The purpose of these organizations was to promote the best possible outcomes for children and their families with home-based and supportive programs. These programs are designed to empower parents to raise resilient, healthy, safe and secure children. They are designed to build and encourage healthy relationships, teach problem-solving skills, support early childhood growth and development, and connect families to important community services. Staff in our program learned about the Apgar,[32] Nipissing[33] and other tests for babies to determine the health and vulnerability of a newborn. Our program was a voluntary program that was offered to mothers at birth. Both parents and parents-to-be could opt into the program to have support navigating their child's early years. The parent(s) would receive information on child development and parent-child interaction. Many mothers in our program had abusive men or had left an abusive man. We were hoping that our program could do one of two things: assist men in learning how to partner and parent without abusing their partner or child(ren), and to ensure that children were not raised in an abusive environment. We wanted to break the cycle of violence and we wanted children to grow up without trauma and abuse.

As the program director, I liked going on periodic visits to homes with staff who were trained in home visitation. This day I was with Jayne, an experienced home visitor. She briefed me on the family and there was one red flag. The male partner had done time for physical assault and while he had visitation rights, he did not have overnight rights and was staying in a homeless shelter. I learned later that he was working and was paying for rent and food for his partner and their two children.

31 See www.ahvna.org

32 The Apgar Score describes the condition of a baby right after birth. The A=Appearance, P=Pulse, G=Grimace Response, A=Activity or muscle tone and R=Respiration rate. See www.acog.org. The Parkin Score also tests for health of a newborn.

33 The Nipissing District Developmental Screen (See www.help.junoemr.com for an excellent explanatory source).

We arrived at the home, and I met mom and the two children. The two-year-old took a fancy to me. As Jayne sat on the couch with the mom and the newborn, I sat on the floor and entertained my new little friend with toys and books. Jayne and the mom were having a good conversation about ACEs (Adverse Childhood Experiences) and they were going over the test that the mom had completed before the visit. The mother was from a racial minority and while ACEs doesn't deal with race, the mom justified some of her own abuse because of her origin. Jayne was in an important conversation when mom's male partner came in from work. He was tall, well built, and had a smile on his face. He kissed his partner, the children, then said hi to Jayne. They knew each other and exchanged pleasantries. He sat down on the floor with me and his two-year-old, and we had a conversation.

He told me about his history of violence from his childhood, about his survival crime as a teen after being forced to leave his home, and about his current situation. He told me that he had pushed his partner which led to the current situation, and he expressed remorse. After we left, Jayne told me that was the first time he had opened up and expressed what he was feeling. She reminded me that her goals were to break the cycle of violence and to see the children grow up happy and well adjusted "so they don't end up in homelessness, addiction, and prison."

Our hope was that over time we would have evidence that rather than ending up in prison, homeless, or addicted, by addressing childhood risk from birth to age six, we would see these children grow into healthy, well-adjusted, and successful adults. When these children become adults, our hope is that an evaluation will show that the cycles of abuse has been broken and participants have not accessed shelters, have not done survival crime, have not been incarcerated, and are leading successful lives.

Conclusion

There are both macro and micro solutions to decriminalizing poverty. This week (December 2023), President Biden in the United States, pardoned thousands of people convicted of marijuana related crimes. Universal Basic Income, building low-income housing, expanding the Drug Courts to other cities, implementing POET programs, expanding programs like

Simon House's addiction treatment and recovery model, are all macro solutions. Sitting on the floor with a dad and a baby talking about issues around trauma and abuse to ensure that the next generation doesn't live with the chaos of their parent's actions is an important micro solution.

Authors

Inès Amzal
European Forum for Urban Security

Carlotta Bauer
TH Köln – University of Applied Sciences

Prof. Dr. Caroline L. Davey
Design Against Crime Solution Centre, University of Salford, UK

Prof. Dr. Alexander Fekete
TH Köln – University of Applied Sciences

Manuela Freiheit
Institute for Interdisciplinary Research on Conflict & Violence (IKG)

Friedrich Gabel
University of Tübingen

Prof. Dr. Christoph Gusy
Bielefeld University

Tjorven Harmsen
University of Freiburg

Prof. Dr. Rita Haverkamp
University of Tübingen

Dr. Dagmar P. Heinrich
Design Against Crime Solution Centre, University of Salford, UK

Chris Hetkämper
TH Köln – University of Applied Sciences

Christoph Kowalewski
Transperency International Germany

Francesc Guillén Lasierra
Departament d'Interior – Generalitat de Catalunya, ES

Dr. John Rook
Simon House Recovery Centre

Pilar De la Torre
European Forum for Urban Security

Andreas Uhl
Institute for Interdisciplinary Research on Conflict & Violence (IKG)

Dr. Macarena Rau Vargas
International CPTED Association

Prof. Dr. Gina Rosa Wollinger
University of Applied Sciences for Police and Public Administration in North Rhine-Westphalia

Prof. Dr. Andrew B. Wootton
Design Against Crime Solution Centre, University of Salford, UK

Prof. Dr. Andreas Zick
Institute for Interdisciplinary Research on Conflict & Violence (IKG)